T0345224

●

CONVERSATIONS

VOLUME 3

Jorge Luis Borges

Osvaldo Ferrari

●

CONVERSATIONS

VOLUME 3

Translated by Anthony Edkins

LONDON NEW YORK CALCUTTA

Seagull Books, 2017

First published as *Reencuentro Diálogos Inéditos*
by Editorial Sudamericana in 1998/1999

© Osvaldo Ferrari, 1999

Published by arrangement with Paterson Marsh Ltd.

English translation © Anthony Edkins, 2017

ISBN 978 0 8574 2 423 5

British Library Cataloguing-in-Publication Data
A catalogue record for this book is available from the British Library

Typeset by Seagull Books, Calcutta, India
Printed and bound by Maple Press, York, Pennsylvania, USA

CONTENTS

BORGES IN OURSELVES, OURSELVES IN BORGES

Osvaldo Ferrari

Fourteen years later, I find myself with them again, hearing the voice of Borges and being amazed, more even than then; these dialogues, doubly unpublished because never before have we dealt with the majority of the themes treated here and because never before have they appeared in book form. They reach up to the last days of our communication in 1985.

Borges is so entirely in them that the encounter leaves me speechless, just like the circular conjunction of his voice, his lucidity and his imagination. On familiarizing myself afresh with this content, I feel myself, as he said in our first dialogues about Yeats, 'wounded, wounded by beauty'.

All of us were awaiting this reencounter with Borges, with the unmistakeable flow of his intelligence and his sensibility; with the inexhaustible weave of his literary passion, his ethical passion and his zenithal perception of everything.

This reencounter is a sum of encounters in which we finally know ourselves, we recognize ourselves and we extend ourselves—Borges in us, ourselves in Borges. As he used to say: 'When we read Shakespeare, we are, if only momentarily, Shakespeare.' In these dialogues, tempered by time, everyone reading them, we are going to be Borges.

Buenos Aires, November 1998

Initial Conversation

9 March 1984

●

OSVALDO FERRARI. Let's begin then, this series of radio conversations. And the first thing I want to ask you, Borges, is how you, who have formed and expressed yourself in the silence of writing, feel about expressing yourself and communicating through the medium of radio.

JORGE LUIS BORGES. I feel a bit nervous. Nevertheless, one spends one's life talking, and here we are, you and I, talking. Writing is occasional and dialogue is continuous, isn't it?

FERRARI. Yes, but it would appear that, for the writer, dialogue is a natural form.

BORGES. Yes, I think so. Moreover, it is something that occurred to Plato, didn't it? He who invented dialogue.

FERRARI. Of course, but unlike musicians and painters, for example . . .

BORGES. Well, they have other means of expression, naturally, but I am limited . . . limited to the word. And, after all, the written word doesn't differ all that much from the oral word.

FERRARI. Now, consider in this epoch in which one thinks or speaks of auditory or visual transmission as a form of communication, if one intuits the listener's presence, as, when writing, one anticipates the presence of the reader . . .

BORGES. Oh, I don't know, when I write, I do it . . . as a relief . . . I like to write. Yes, that doesn't mean I believe in the value of what I write, but, yes, in the pleasure of writing. I mean, if I were Robinson Crusoe, I believe I'd write on my island.

FERRARI. I understand.

BORGES. Without thinking of readers.

FERRARI. Without thinking of readers.

BORGES. Yes, I never think about the reader, except in the sense of trying to write in a comprehensible way—it's a simple act of politeness, although it is towards persons completely imaginary or absent. I don't believe that confusion is a merit.

FERRARI. And do you believe that without thinking of communication, suddenly communication, of which so much is spoken, can be produced?

BORGES. No, I don't think about communication. When I write something, it is because I have received something. That means I believe, humbly, in inspiration. That is to say, every writer is an amanuensis. An amanuensis doesn't know who or what. We can think, as did the

Hebrews, of the ruaj, the spirit, or of the muse as did the Greeks, or of the 'great memory' as did the Irish poet William Butler Yeats . . . he believed that every writer inherited the memory of his elders, in other words, the human race, since we have two parents, four grandparents, et cetera, multiplying themselves in geometric progression. He thought that a writer himself cannot have many experiences but can count on that vast past . . . 'the great memory'. We can call it 'the subconscious' as well, but 'the great memory' is nicer, isn't it?, an inexhaustible spring.

FERRARI. Of course.

BORGES. But the idea is the same, it's the idea of receiving something, recalling something.

FERRARI. But you have spoken precisely of something that is increasingly mentioned less. I recall that on receiving an important prize in Spain, you said that if the spirit has managed to transmit something through you to others, then you feel that your destiny has been fulfilled.

BORGES. I feel justified. My only possible destiny is the literary destiny. For a man who has committed the imprudence of reaching eighty-four, who soon will be eighty-five, who is blind . . . well, the majority of my contemporaries have died, although, as you see, there are young people surrounding my old age. I spend some part of my time alone and then I people it with projects. For example, this morning I woke at seven, I knew they were going to call me at half past eight. I thought: Good, let's take advantage of this time. And I began, mentally, you understand, to smudge a sonnet which in a few days' time will really be a sonnet. Now it's merely a rough draft. So, I spend a good part of my time alone, and I have to people it with projects, with mysteries we could say, except it sounds a bit horrific, amazing doesn't it? But I don't feel threatened by them, they are pleasant mysteries.

FERRARI. I understand, but this idea you have of the muse, of the spirit . . . in an epoch in which the notion of the spirit presiding over the movement of art or literature would seem to have been lost.

BORGES. No, I don't think so, eh? I believe that every writer feels that he receives. That is to say, he can't give if he hasn't received. Now I've reached another conclusion which doesn't contradict what I've just said—no, rather, it complements, and that is: it's better to intervene as little as possible in your work. Above all, it's better that my opinion doesn't intervene. To write is a way of dreaming, and one has to try to dream sincerely. One knows that everything is false— but it is true for one. That is to say, when I write I am dreaming, I know that I am dreaming, but I try to dream sincerely.

FERRARI. There is something true. The truth that we are given, that we receive, as you say.

BORGES. Yes, I believe that we are continually receiving. What's more, I also believe, and I have said this many times, that if one were really a poet, and I am sure I am not one, or am one very rarely, one would feel each instant as poetic, each moment of life. That idea that there are poetic themes and prosaic themes is an error, for everything must be felt as poetic. I believe that some poets, for example Walt Whitman, got to feel that, to feel that each moment of his life was no less divine, or—because divine is a very ambitious word—no less astonishing, no less interesting than others.

FERRARI. But . . .

BORGES. Just now, for example, is pretty unusual. We are conversing, you and I, and at the same time, you have told me we are surrounded by multitudes, invisible and future . . . maybe even hypothetical. It's quite poetic, isn't it?—that idea that, really, we are not alone, that we are surrounded by an amphitheatre of future people.

FERRARI. Yes, but you observed that this conception of yours—of the creation as something that is received by whoever writes or creates— is an idea, in some way, mystical.

BORGES. Yes, it can be.

FERRARI. Because there would be waiting, and there would be a receiver, and there would be an expectancy from it.

BORGES. I believe so.

FERRARI. I have sometimes thought that the process of being a poet or a writer seems like that of a mystic.

BORGES. Very well, but why not be a mystic? At any rate, I believe that being a mystic is inoffensive.

FERRARI. I ask it because . . .

BORGES. Yes, I know, because now we are confusing literature, shall we say, with journalism, or with history.

FERRARI. Clearly.

BORGES. But I believe it isn't so, I believe that one isn't trying to refer to facts . . . well, I don't know if we are using the right word, since everything is true. But, in the end, we are not trying to refer to things that happen . . . to me . . . and to my imagination, I should say . . .

FERRARI. Exactly. With reference to your imagination and to your memory—there are many people who wonder about your imagination, in that everything seems to find itself, in that everything seems to fit. What can it tell us of your imagination and of your memory?

BORGES. Well, I believe, like the Jewish-French philosopher Bergson, that the memory is selective, and that one chooses . . . memory chooses. Therefore, one tends to forget disagreeable facts. I know that I spent eleven days, with their nights, in a sanatorium, in the month of February, I was on my back, couldn't move, could lose sight if I moved. Well, I know that because they have told me about it, but really, those eleven days and those eleven nights of intolerable heat and forced immobility are in my memory a single instant. However, they must have been terrible when they happened. And now I recount it as if it had happened to another. On the other hand, I like to think of the moments of happiness, and perhaps sometimes I exaggerate the happiness of those moments, since it's pleasant to recall them.

FERRARI. Is it, in some way, the memory of your character, Dhalman, in the story 'The South', the memory of those eleven days?

BORGES. That's right . . . of course, yes. I refer to another operation, since I've spent a large part of my life in sanatoriums. But that doesn't matter because I've forgotten them. For example, when they performed an operation on me in a sanatorium in Palermo, a long operation and a long convalescence in a sanatorium in Brasil Street, near Constitución. But I know them as facts, not as personal experiences. I mean, I know them in the same way, well, as I know my Borges grandfather fought in the battle of Caseros when he was sixteen. That is, it is something that I have heard.

FERRARI. But do you believe then, that one cultivates the memory? You have made in some way a process through which you have cultivated your memory in time. Because it would seem to be a memory that has developed itself particularly..

BORGES. And I believe my blindness has helped me.

FERRARI. Oh, I understand.

BORGES. Of course, if I were to recover my sight, I would not leave this house, I would read these books that surround us, that are so near and so far. Unfortunately I am forbidden the reading of those books—I can only hear them read. And there is a big difference, since the fact of leafing a book is denied me. Someone comes here, I beg him to read me something, well he duly reads to me . . . but the fact of leafing a book, being omitted, being skipped, that is denied me, naturally, and that is part of the pleasure of reading.

FERRARI. But, then, blindness has perhaps beautifully contributed to your memory and your imagination.

BORGES. In any case, if that's not so, I must try to think it so. I must believe that blindness is something like everything in the world, that it too is a gift. And, of course, we already know that misfortune is a gift, since from misfortune tragedy has come perhaps . . . and . . . almost all of poetry. I don't know if unhappiness is useful, in that sense. Happiness is an end in itself, unhappiness is not. The duty of an artist, of any artist—would I were a musician, or a painter, like my sister . . . but no, I am a writer— is the transmutation into something different of those things that happen to him. Naturally, in my case, I'm limited by words and, moreover, my destiny is the Castilian tongue. And, well, I must try to do what I can within those means and within that tradition, since each language is a tradition. I wrote a poem this morning, and one of the themes of the poem is that languages are not equivalent, that each language is a new way of feeling the world. Currently I'm trying to know some Japanese, and the difficulty is not in memorizing the words but that I feel everything in that world is a long way away from me. Although I like it very much, and I spent maybe the happiest five weeks of my life in Japan, every day a gift. I got to know seven cities, people were extraordinarily polite. And with María Kodama, we visited temples, gardens, rivers, sanctuaries.

FERRARI. As you are going to do again shortly.

BORGES. Yes. I conversed with monks and nuns of the Buddhist faith and of the Shinto. I never thought that that were possible, but I was conversing with them. That seemed to me incredible.

FERRARI. Imagination confronted reality at that moment.

BORGES. Yes, I had got to think that at my age nothing new could happen to me, that I had exhausted the number of my experiences, that it only remained for me to repeat them. But then that splendid gift turned up—an invitation to Japan, by the Japan Foundation, to spend four weeks. Those four weeks were to be five. I told them not to disclose anything to me, that I wanted each day to be a surprise and that surprise could be, well, a Buddhist sanctuary, it could be a garden. Those small Japanese gardens were not made for strolling in but to be seen, where rock and water are more important than vegetation. And then I had the opportunity to talk to writers too.

FERRARI. It would seem to have been a sort of correspondence with the imagination throughout time.

BORGES. Yes.

FERRARI. But there has been another inexhaustible thing about you, Borges, which is mentioned in Buenos Aires as unique—I refer to wit. People are accustomed to listen through means of communication to a witty Borges . . .

BORGES. No, I'm not witty or at least I don't try to be so . . .

FERRARI. I speak of literary wit . . .

BORGES. When I'm talking, I'm thinking aloud—but I'm not trying to be witty. And plays on words I find unpleasant . . .

FERRARI. But when the witty borders humour, politics . . .

BORGES. Ah, that is something else.

FERRARI. Society, literature, one is dealing with a witty vision of the world.

BORGES. Oh yes, it can be. Would it were not, in my case . . .

FERRARI. And maybe wit and genius are slightly similar.

BORGES. Well, genius seems a very ambitious word. Witty seems somewhat vain, doesn't it? I don't want to be witty.

FERRARI. To set out to be witty, not in any way, but you are without setting out to be so.

BORGES. Verbally, let's say, no. Now, things occur to me, yes. But inventions occur to me more than plays on words, which personally I detest. Although I like rhyme, which is, strictly speaking, a game of words (*laughs*).

FERRARI. I understand.

BORGES. Rather, a game about the poetic possibilities of words. They say that rhymes are always the same, and one must seek, however, different associations, and one already knows that after sombra, nombra, no?

FERRARI. True. For this first time, Borges, we have to say goodbye to the listeners . . .

BORGES. Good Lord, what a pity . . .

FERRARI. To re-encounter them, next Friday . . .

BORGES. But we've only been talking for three minutes . . .

FERRARI. True, it seems there have been no more than three minutes. But time has run out.

BORGES. Well, many thanks.

FERRARI. Thanks to you.

BORGES. No, thanks to you, thanks.

2

Stevenson and Bunyan

●

OSVALDO FERRARI. In that book you compiled with Adolfo Bioy Casares, *The Book of Heaven and Hell*, I find a fragment of Stevenson called 'against heaven'. And it begins by saying: 'Happiness, eternal or temporary, is not the recompense that man seeks . . . '

JORGE LUIS BORGES. Well, Shaw says something similar in *Major Barbara*: 'I have freed myself from the bribery of heaven.' So that's the same idea, isn't it?

FERRARI. It coincides, precisely.

BORGES. But it can also mean another thing, it can mean that happiness is not enough, that an effort is necessary. Because there's a poem by Tennyson in which he speaks of the soul, and says that it does not desire to rest in a golden heaven but wants 'the work of going on and not to die'. What he wants is to be permitted to continue—and not to die. What the soul wants is activity itself, work I suppose, don't you agree?

FERRARI. Clearly, an eternal way of being.

BORGES. Yes, to be eternal but not lazily, to be eternal by forcing oneself to work.

FERRARI. Then Stevenson adds: 'I would not say it aloud; for man's cherished belief is that he loves that happiness which he continually spurns and passes by; and this belief in some ulterior happiness exactly fits him. He does not require to stop and taste it; he can be about the rugged and bitter business where his heart lies; and yet he can tell himself this fairy tale of an eternal tea party, and enjoy the notion that he is both himself and something else; and that his friends will yet meet him, all ironed out and emasculate, and still be lovable . . . '

BORGES (*laughs*). Yes, I remember that last phrase. Well, I suppose that the conversation in that social gathering to which Stevenson refers will be a long dialogue without arguments, don't you think, a kind of vague harmony, an infinite social gathering. I mean, Stevenson knew that that wasn't able to enchant but that hope could satisfy. Not the realization of it, or the fulfilment of desire—the important thing was that desire itself. Now, the title ('Against Heaven') no doubt isn't that. Bioy Casares surely invented it, because we had to put a title, and that is a fragment of a long essay, naturally.

FERRARI. It comes in the letters of Stevenson.

BORGES. Ah, of course.

FERRARI. But the last phrase is also very interesting. It ends with: 'As if love does not nourish itself with the defects of the loved one.'

BORGES. That's right, and that is from his collected letters. The *Collected Letters* of 1886.

FERRARI. It appears that over time, Borges, Stevenson's letters have been transmitted by you to others in Buenos Aires.

BORGES. Yes, I think I told you that one of the most pleasant facts of my life—which happened to me a little while ago—was when I ran across a boy in the street, and he said to me: 'I want to thank you for something, Borges.' 'What?' I asked him, and he said: 'You got me to know Robert Luis Stevenson.' And I thought: In that case, I feel justified. I don't know what he was called, I don't know anything about him. And that was so perfect, for what would be added by proper names?

FERRARI. The testimony suffices.

BORGES. The testimony suffices and Stevenson's name suffices perfectly too. Because if he had said: You've made me know Milton or Shakespeare, the phrase would not have had any force, would it?, not any efficacy. The point is the fact of referring to a writer as likeable as Stevenson.

FERRARI. You also said to me regarding Stevenson that in several countries, including our own, his magnitude is not appreciated because he, and many others too, is associated with children's stories.

BORGES. Yes, it's dangerous for a writer to write for children because it's thought that everything he wrote was written for children. So that, for example, for Kipling's fame, it has not helped to have written the *Just So Stories* or *The Jungle Book*, because he is judged for those only. There are other cases. Let's take the example of Lewis Carroll—it's usual to think that the two volumes of *Alice in Wonderland* are for children. Well, they are for children but they are also for grown-ups.

But it doesn't matter, the childish quality in those texts is what's insisted on.

FERRARI. And in Stevenson's case, he's immediately linked with *Treasure Island.*

BORGES. Yes, maybe it's not convenient for Silvino Ocampo to have written that very beautiful book (*La naranja maravillosa*), because anyone who has read that book will judge her in terms of that book and will think the others are likewise. And they are no less gorgeous but they are completely different.

FERRARI. Well, she had the luck of having written them in, let's say, a very late stage of her work. That is to say, she was known before by her stories and the poems.

BORGES. But I don't know if she is known well enough.

FERRARI. Ah no, you're right.

BORGES. I think it's called Exaltation of the Cross, and they asked me to name the best contemporary Argentinian writer. So I spoke of Silvina Ocampo but I understood that name meant nothing. They listening, true, but later somebody supposed that it was a mistake, that I had wanted to say Victoria Ocampo and I had got the name wrong. I had to explain to him, no. In the end, that name seems not have acquired the echo, the resonance and the ambit it deserved.

FERRARI. The same mistake is always made with her.

BORGES. Yes.

FERRARI. Of associating her with Victoria Ocampo.

BORGES. And of seeing her in terms of her older sister, of Victoria.

FERRARI. And of her marriage with Bioy Casares, and of her friendship with Borges.

BORGES. Well, I don't know if she has thought of the last. Yes, she can of course be thought of as the younger sister of Victoria, wife of Bioy Casares . . . and she stops being counted.

FERRARI (*laughs*). This book I referred to, the *Book of Heaven and Hell*, was it done with the idea of bringing together a selection of texts linked to the theme of heaven and hell?

BORGES. What we were seeking is an heterogeneous and picturesque book, and I believe it is both things.

FERRARI. It certainly is and, what's more, it's very varied—a large quantity of authors is cited.

BORGES. Among them mystics such as Swedenborg.

FERRARI. Yes.

BORGES. There are texts by him. And the references to heaven and hell are many . . . But I believe we did not include any Dantean passage. Why? Because it is too evident or because we had to quote it in Castilian, and we understood that the text, translated, lost something, since it seems impossible that a book of heaven and hell disregards Hell and Paradise, no?

FERRARI. On the other hand, there is another English writer, linked with mysticism—John Bunyan.

BORGES. Ah, Bunyan. I think we record the last page of the *Pilgrim's Progress*, don't we?

FERRARI. Certainly, which is marvellous.

BORGES. And that gentleman who is called Valiant-for-the-truth.

FERRARI. Precisely: 'whose pitcher has been broken on top of the fountain'.

BORGES. Yes, that passage we quoted was cited by Shaw too, in which he says that Bunyan is more drastic than Shakespeare. Possibly Shaw wanted to scandalize a little also, don't you think?, since 'more than Shakespeare' is something which is hard to admit in England. Although many people feel so, it is seen as slightly heretical or as pleasantly heretical.

FERRARI. I'm interested to know your opinion of that book, so famous in English literature, *The Pilgrim's Progress*.

BORGES. It's an allegory, but to enjoy that book one must forget that it is an allegory, and perhaps that can be said of every allegory. That is to say, if one thinks that those characters correspond to the names that they have—they are, for example, called Mr Hypocrite, Mr Liar—if one reads the book in that way, one can let oneself be captivated by that reading.

FERRARI. How would you translate the title?

BORGES. I think you would have to say 'El camino del peregrino'— 'The Way of the Pilgrim', but it doesn't sound good. Progress for 'progreso', clearly no . . . route, way, I don't know. The route of the pilgrim? Perhaps most important for each word is its context, more than the word itself.

FERRARI. In North America, this book is studied in the university.

BORGES. It's a very easy book and very pleasant reading, and it's all based on biblical texts. For example, in the edition I have, one reads in the margin: Ecclesiastes, chapter such-and-such, verse such-and-such. So that book, which has so much its own life, has nevertheless come from a series of quotations.

FERRARI. That will have something to do with the mystical character that is attributed to Bunyan.

BORGES. Yes, I've read other books by him and his autobiography in which he sees himself as a terrible sinner, though the sins he confesses to aren't so terrible. But he had a sense of guilt. And now, one of the beautiful phrases, of which we have once spoken, was about his father, who was a baker, and he says: 'My father was a baker of human bread.' One feels that he is good, doesn't one? Moreover, bread has a tradition other food doesn't have.

FERRARI. Bread can be associated with meat especially.

BORGES. Yes, in the Lord's Prayer: 'Give us this day our daily bread'. I want to say food. And there's a Protestant sect, I don't know which, that translates it as: 'Give of this day our supernatural bread.' I suppose it implies that one does not request a nourishing gift but a spiritual one.

FERRARI. Naturally.

BORGES. How odd that you should speak to me about this. I've been leafing through the nine history books of Herodotus. It seems there was an argument between the Pelagians and the Egyptians about which was the most ancient nation, and they resolved to do an experiment: to take two children who were brought up first by a priest, and then by two women whose tongues had been ripped out. And the first word they said was a word which I don't now remember but which in Pelagian—not in Egyptian—meant bread. And then one sees: that was the primitive language of humanity.

3

Chance

●

OSVALDO FERRARI. More than magic, more than revolution, more than miracle, you seem to believe, Borges, in chance, in that physical law that you extend to the spiritual plane.

JORGE LUIS BORGES. Yes, but the law is quite mysterious too. It's now known why certain causes have to produce a determined effect. Nevertheless, I dogmatically believe in it, although I can't explain it. Just recently you said that to me and I realized that law is arbitrary. Well, magic comes to be a form, an extension of the law of chance, doesn't it? And superstition as well.

FERRARI. Enlargements . . .

BORGES. Yes, for example, if thirteen guests sit down at a table, one of them may die that year. . . . De Quincey found an explanation or pseudo-explanation of that law—I believe the Stoics also use it—and it's this: if one supposes that the universe constitutes a single organism, then there is a necessary relationship between each of its parts, and it can well have a relationship between the fact of spilling salt, breaking a mirror, walking under a ladder, thirteen sitting down at the same table, and some fact that occurs later . . . Now, I think two things are usually confused. For example, let's take the case of astrology: it's supposed there is a relationship between the configuration of the stars and the fact that a man may be engendered at such-and-such a stage of that configuration. That comes to be the base of astrology. But it is one thing to admit that relationship exists, and another that one can find out about it or study it.

Of course, if the universe is one, as De Quincey says, lesser things are secret mirrors of the greater, everything is linked. But to establish that link seems much more difficult. Without doubt, there's a relationship between a page written by me and my character. That's a matter of graphology, but to study that relationship seems to me extremely difficult. Both things are confused. It is supposed that one admits the relationship can be investigated. But already a difficulty arises . . . I'm ready to admit there's a relationship between all the facts of the universe or, anyway, that it's not illogical to suppose so. But the fact that this relationship can be studied, that seems to me much harder. Or, seeking newer examples of superstitions, doubtless there's a relationship between each individual and the dreams that he has . . .

FERRARI. Anyway, you are not disposed to accept the omnipotence of psychology or sociology.

BORGES. No, but that a person's infirmity can be cured by studying his dreams, seems to me more difficult. That the relationship exists, I'm ready to admit, but the links between an infirmity a man suffers from and his dreams has to be so complex and so ramified that I don't know if they can be studied. I mean I don't know if a psychiatrist can cure a sick person even if dreams have some relation with that sickness, if that sickness is, above all, mental.

FERRARI. Of course, one is dealing with two different aspects. But, getting back to chance, it seems to me you believe it is not necessarily determined by a God or by a transcendental power.

BORGES. No, one could think in all previous universal history, or—to employ more ambitious words—in all the previous cosmic processes. Doubtless everything is related but that this may be unravelled seems to me beyond human intelligence and, perhaps, a conjectural divine intelligence.

FERRARI. That the origin may be unravelled.

BORGES. Clearly, precisely. Now, if it exists, why not?

FERRARI. In what seems to me a certainty in you is the idea of predestination—the relation between chance and predetermination. To the fact that those causes and those effects are predestined to occur in a certain way.

BORGES. Yes, but that someone knows that predestination or that someone fixes it is different, isn't it? In the case of Calvinism, or the Puritanism that proceeds, the idea that somebody is predestined to heaven or to hell—if these posthumous institutions exist—well, that seems more difficult. That is to say, there may be predestination, but that someone knows that . . . of course, an infinite intelligence is by definition capable of everything, but I don't know if the phrase 'infinite intelligence' has any sense or is simply an abuse, or a distraction of the language.

FERRARI. That is to say, neither in respect to chance nor in respect to predestination can we know if something or someone determines them.

BORGES. Yes, and they can exist beyond an individual expert in them.

FERRARI. Talking of religions. Could we think that men believe in a religion or a mythology according to the spiritual or magical climate in which they are immersed? Let's take the case of Plato: the Greeks could have understood it in their time, because in Greek life, poetry and philosophy were a form of reality.

BORGES. Yes, but I don't know up to where it was thought that words like Eros corresponded to a being or was a metaphor for something. That we shall never know, and it will be varied according to believers or sceptics. You will see, for example, in Latin one says *Sub Jove* (under Jupiter) which means in the elements, which indicates that in some way Jupiter signified space. A little like Spinoza with his *Deus sive natura*, isn't it? God or nature.

FERRARI. Yes, now that spiritual or magical climate in which things are more credible, it can be a given, according to conjecture, among Christ's contemporaries, who could have seen and recognized, having the gaze prepared to see it. Spiritually prepared, let's say.

BORGES. And, maybe, the more simple the people, the easier it was to admit that. My father told me that the bishop of Paraná went all over the province of Entre Ríos. And then, that individual, who arrived dressed in black in an important carriage, caught the attention of the *paisanos*. And then, when he went from one place, or from a ranch, the gauchos discussed that he who had been there was Bishop of

Paraná—or God (*both laugh*). But, as my father said to me: possibly for those gauchos, both words didn't amount to a very important difference. Because now we think of the bishop of Paraná as an ecclesiastical functionary, and God as the creator of heaven and earth who lives in eternity and not in the temporal. But who knows if these distinctions existed for the gauchos of 1880, in the province of Entre Ríos. Perhaps that discussion was purely verbal, don't you think?

FERRARI. Definitely. I've chosen a poem of yours, Borges, in which I think one encounters your idea of predestation. We're talking about 'The Labyrinth'—I don't know if you remember it.

BORGES. I fear having written it, if you were to read it to me, I could identify it. Or not.

FERRARI. I propose to read it.

BORGES. Good, we have time for fourteen lines?

FERRARI (*laughs*). I think so. 'The Labyrinth' says: 'Zeus could not undo the stone nets that encircle me . . . '

BORGES. The one who speaks, who is it? Theseus or the Minotaur?

FERRARI. That's what I wanted to ask you.

BORGES. Ah, good, we'll find out.

FERRARI. 'Of stone that encircles me. I have forgotten / the men who before I was; I follow the hated / way of monotonous walls that is my destiny. Straight galleries / that curve in secret circles / after all the years . . . '

BORGES. Of course. Those verses give the idea that the labyrinth is vast—the curve seems a straight line, and one doesn't visually notice the curve. That is, what he sees, because the wall is so vast, is a straight line but, really, there's a slight curve and it's part of a circle.

FERRARI. He continues, saying: 'Parapets / have been worn smooth by the passage of days. / Here in the tepid alabaster dust / are tracks that frighten me. The hollow air / of evening sometimes brings a bellowing, / or the echo, desolate, of bellowing. / I know that hidden in the shadows there / lurks another, whose task is to exhaust / the loneliness that braids and weaves this hell, / to crave my blood, and to fatten on my death. / We seek each other. Oh, if only this / were the last day of our antithesis!'

BORGES. Good, now that we've reached the end of the sonnet, I don't know if we're dealing with Theseus, the Minotaur, or with someone who is both. Then the poem would be the richer, if the subject were Theseus or the Minotaur, or, better, Theseus and the Minotaur. Because there it seems that a lot of time has gone by, and that time seems to correspond more to the Minotaur who is the Labyrinth's inhabitant, than to Theseus who, in the end, is an explorer, isn't he?

FERRARI. A visitor.

BORGES. A visitor, an explorer, good, perhaps the poem turns out better . . . let's leave it vague. What's more, why try an explanation? What I say won't be worth more than the poem itself, which will go on being read, and continue ramifying in a way, good, almost as vast as the labyrinth with which it deals.

FERRARI. I bring it up as an example of your vision of predestination, but I now think it's one of your most original poems. I don't know if you'll agree with me.

BORGES. In this moment you've revealed it to me, I really like it. Above all, I like the vagueness about who is speaking in it.

4

Fantastic Literature and Science Fiction

●

*Proposed by the Italian critic Lucio D'Arcangelo and by the writer Ángel Bonomini, Osvaldo Ferrari asked Jorge Luis Borges the following questions.*s

OSVALDO FERRARI. What would be the fundamental differences between realist fiction and fantastic fiction?

JORGE LUIS BORGES. Since we don't know if the universe belongs to the realist genre or to the fantastic genre, the difference would be, above all, in the reader, and in the writer's intention. But, of course, according to idealism, everything is fantastic or everything is real. It would come to be the same.

FERRARI. Referring to our century, some speak of the fantastic without intellectual or metaphysical ghosts, and finally of a fantastic discourse very close to paradox. What's your opinion about this?

BORGES. The first Argentinian writer who deliberately cultivated the fantastic genre is, I think, Leopoldo Lugones with *Las fuerzas extrañas* (Strange Forces). Certainly, in *Isur*, there are no ghosts. There is that fantastic story of the monkey who, trying to talk, drives himself mad.

And that book we are accustomed to forget, published in the first decade of the twentieth century, although it was a book which didn't play with the decorative prose of the modernists or the deliberately archaic prose of those who imitated the Spanish, a book which went more or less unnoticed. And of course, a great book in the *Antología de la literature fantastica* which Silvina Ocampo, Bioy Casares and I edited, we included not that story but 'Los caballos de Abdera' whose point of departure is a sonnet by . . . Heredia.

FERRARI. How do you explain, they ask, the renaissance of fantastic literature in Argentina?

BORGES. I don't know. I suppose I'm one of the guilty (*both laugh*). But it's natural that I be guilty, since one of my first readings was, well, Poe's stories, and those unforgettable nightmares of Wells—*The Time Machine, The Island of Doctor Moreau, The First Man on the Moon, The Invisible Man* . . . And I went back to all that in my first fantastic stories.

FERRARI. There are those who imagine that in future there will be no place for fantastic literature . . .

BORGES. Why not?

FERRARI. That it will be replaced by science fiction. Do you share this opinion?

BORGES. First: 'ciencia ficción', 'science fiction' is a bad translatio. Because when there are compound words in English, the first has the value of an adjective, so *science fiction* would have, in good grammar, in good logic, to be translated as 'scientific fiction'—and not 'science fiction' which is absurd. Because, for example, if you say *water fall*, you do not translate it as 'agua caida' but as 'caida de agua'. I don't know how they have fallen into that error—everybody speaks of 'science fiction' and that is absurd. It is scientific fiction, it is not a compound word. Good, but what was the question, because I've got lost in etymologies (*both laugh*).

FERRARI. If you think it will replace fantastic literature . . .

BORGES. No, why should it? I believe in the inferiority of scientific fiction. Because, for example, if they tell us that if a man puts on a ring, as in the 'Volsunga saga', he becomes invisible, they demand a single act of faith. On the other hand, if they tell us he has to submerge himself in a special liquid which has to be wine, that he has to be nude so that he does not see the rope, as in the admirable 'invisible man' of Wells, then they demand several acts of faith. And we think, moreover, why did the author not invent that apparatus. In the other case, they ask us for a single act of faith, already traditional, that of a magic object, and we easily accept it. So I believe that, maybe with time, one turns to the system of a single magic object, a single act of faith, and not successive acts of laborious laboratories. I believe it's simpler to accept a ring than a laboratory. At least for me, who knows nothing of science.

In the end, science fiction would be a genre of fantastic fiction, nothing more. There's no need to oppose it.

FERRARI. In a way, they say, literature could be if not defined then at least delimited by its thematic possibilities. Could you talk to us about the thematics of fantastic literature?

BORGES. I suppose that thematics means the theme, but now they pre-fer proparoxytone words, don't they?, and long words: 'methodology' instead of 'method', 'thematics' instead of 'theme' . . . I suppose they are the themes of all literature. For example, Wells, in his auto-biography, says he felt very alone, he was a young boy, tubercular, he arrived in London from Kent, he was very poor. And that later, to signify that loneliness, he wrote *The Invisible Man*. But previously the source was his solitude. That is to say, the sources of fantastic litera-ture are those of all literature—emotion, shall we say?

FERRARI. Of course.

BORGES. And without it, you can't write. I don't know why people like so much the idea that a machine can write poems. Well, it's not impossible that it does, but what need does a machine have to write them? None. If I feel emotion, good, I can give vent to it by my own means—but not by putting in motion a series of screws.

5

James Joyce

●

OSVALDO FERRARI. There's a book and an author, Borges, who in spite of their vast renown remain unfathomable to the majority of the readers. I refer to James Joyce and his *Ulysses*.

JORGE LUIS BORGES. Possibly it was made to be unfathomable. It was made to be commented on. I think it was written as an experiment, destined to be a bit secret, or, more important, it was the mechanism. Because I've read that book by Stuart Gilbert, which is like a plan of *Ulysses*, and it is a reading somewhat more delightful than *Ulysses*, which perhaps can't be read without that plan. For example, in that book, the rhetorical figure predominating each chapter is indicated. It seems that in each chapter one colour predominates. Let's say, red. And then, in each of the chapters, in each episode a reference is made to a body function—so, in the case of red, it has to be the circulation of the blood. And then the exact hour of what occurs in that scene is given, so that one can compare that chapter which corresponds to the mind of Stephen Dedalus with another which corresponds to the mind of Leopold Bloom. And then there is a moment in which the two of them fix on a cloud. One understands that this parallelism is precious. What's more, each episode corresponds with episodes of *The Odyssey* . . . it is understood that there are parallel lives. And then, the technique that is employed . . . I think there's a chapter in which all forms of the metaphor are used, and there's a list of those forms, and there are examples of synecdoches, metonymy, whatever. And yet another in which the idea of questions and answers is pursued—catechism, interrogation. And then, the final one, which is the most famous: Molly's interior monologue, thirty or forty pages without punctuation, corresponding to the flow of consciousness, although it has been signalled that the consciousness flows without using words, that is to say, one goes on feeling or thinking things but not thinking the words which correspond to those things. That is to say, that the flow of consciousness has to reject language, or, in every case, verbs could be used, but nothing else. On the other hand, there are out there adjectives, nouns, prepositions, conjunctions and, furthermore, phrases.

FERRARI. Which makes possible interpretation extremely difficult.

BORGES. I don't believe he wrote it so that it could be . . .

FERRARI. Interpreted.

BORGES. Yes, or enjoyed. I believe it's as if it were a kind of *reductio ad absurdum* of all literature, including the realist novel.

FERRARI. Of course.

BORGES. Yes, I think the idea is something akin to it carrying all tradition . . . carrying it much further and finally destroying it. I would say that of *Ulysses*, but then along came *Finnegan's Wake* . . . They are facts, let's say, to finish literature, to be the end of literature. I suppose he thought that after that nothing could be written, because all that is written would come to be like a projection, or a useless repetition of those books. In other words, I think Joyce wrote those books to be the last books. But people haven't thought so, on the contrary—he has disciples, and literature continues in spite of those books which are believed to be the final milestones of literature.

Now, it's undeniable that Joyce had an infinite . . . yes, let's say, an infinite verbal capacity, and, moreover, the English language permitted it, although more difficult than German to mint compound words. Now, I don't know how Joyce participated in the French version of *Ulysses*, along with Valéry Larbaud, Stuart Gilbert and others, because he knew that a good part of the structure of his book, well, had its origin in compound words, and because of that, was untranslatable.

FERRARI. What's more, he was a master of neologisms.

BORGES. Now that, without doubt in the German version you can do, because in German compound words are so usable that people coin them in conversation. You can mint compound words in the dialogue, and that disturbs nobody, because one immediately understands. On the other hand, they are artificial in English, and in Spanish they are impossible.

FERRARI. So Joyce could have realized literature's last judgement in *Finnegan's Wake* and in *Ulysses*.

BORGES. Above all in *Finnegan's Wake*, a last extension of *Ulysses*. It seems that after that there can no longer be literature. However, literature has continued, using those conventions. Particularly the interior monologue, that has been much used. I think there are two literal translations of *Ulysses* but they're fairly ugly, because what's been translated is the sense. The Castilian words are very long and the effect of Joyce is, above all, the effect of his cadences which have been lost in this case. The literal translation has taken into account simply the sense, and not considered that, in English, it shapes like verse, at any rate, it possesses cadences very, very pleasant to the ear. In a literal translation, the result is simply clumsy phrases, and the compound words become artificial or over-elaborate. In English, they become somewhat artificial. Whereas in German they don't—in German you can be continually coining words and nobody minds, it doesn't arrest the reader. In contrast, in English they fairly rare. In Castilian, or in the romance languages they are impossible.

FERRARI. So the contemporary novel, instead of ending with Joyce, utilized or took advantage of Joyce.

BORGES. Yes.

FERRARI. It incorporated him.

BORGES. Yes, which is not what he expected, I believe.

FERRARI. Or what he wanted.

BORGES. I believe that he wanted to be the last, no? He had wanted the death of the novel.

FERRARI. Yes.

BORGES. It is what he had looked for. He had already written some very pretty poems, but they were short poems, with exquisite cadences that were no danger to poetry. In contrast, those two novels, yes, they are a kind of *reductio ad absurdum*, since they don't excuse a moment of the twenty-four hours of the two characters: each instant is registered, even the least memorable ones. Don't you agree?

FERRARI. In those moments of that single day in which everything is developed.

BORGES. Yes, and it is understood that on that single day, the chronicle of that day but also that chronicle in some way of the *Odyssey*. That is to say, what requires many years in the *Odyssey* is supposed to take place in the conscience of two characters, and he chooses a random day, an arbitrary day, and he situates it in Dublin . . . of course, because Joyce lived in nostalgia for Dublin. And he never wanted to return . . .

FERRARI. Yes.

BORGES. Perhaps nostalgia is a way of possessing things.

FERRARI. And he wrote *Dubliners*.

BORGES. And he also wrote *Dubliners*. Or perhaps he thought, well, to have written those books was to be in Dublin. Physical presence wasn't necessary.

FERRARI. Oh, of course.

BORGES. And he was already there without those books.

FERRARI. Certainly, literary evocation was more effective thus.

BORGES. It's that to feel nostalgia, one has to be far away. Maybe he would have thought of the Jews in Jerusalem if there had been no exodus, and then . . . what's the word?

FERRARI. Diaspora.

BORGES. And through the diaspora, clearly. If it had not been for the exodus and the diaspora, they would not have constructed that image of Jerusalem and the nostalgia for Jerusalem. The exodus and the diaspora, of course, and Israel is actually a state. Doubtless, Jerusalem will lose that magic prestige, which had been impossible . . . now it's no longer impossible. And that for poetry is a loss, isn't it? The fact that one can no longer talk about Jerusalem, because one can catch a steamer, or a train, and arrive. It was a magic city, wasn't it?

FERRARI. Yes. Now, getting back to Joyce: it's evident the incidence of the religious upbringing in him. We see it especially in *Portrait of the Artist as a Young Man*.

BORGES. Yes, because there he repudiates the Catholic faith, but in some way . . . the word atheist, I believe it varies for each religion. That is to say, if I'm an atheist within Protestantism, it's not the same as being an atheist within the Catholic faith or within Judaism. It has a different meaning. Because it disregards or denies a God who is essentially diverse, essentially distinct.

FERRARI. But this incidence of religious upbringing, I think it's translated in all of Joyce's work. You yourself once said that all days were, in some way, secret, the irreparable day of Justice for him, all the sites of hell and purgatory.

BORGES. And, if it is not, then *Ulysses* has no sense.

FERRARI. Clearly.

BORGES. I say: Why has *Ulysses* been written if it is supposed that something has been excluded from that day and from that book? One gathers that book is a kind of microcosm, isn't it?, and it covers the world . . . although, because it's fairly extensive, I don't believe anyone has read it (*both laugh*). Many people have analysed it. Now, as for reading the book from the beginning to the end—I don't know if anyone has done it.

FERRARI. Even having done so, it would have been impossible to stay integrally registered in the reader's memory.

BORGES. And one would have to suppose an infinite memory. Well, maybe many books are written not in terms of each page but in the memory that they leave, no?

FERRARI. Of course.

BORGES. Possibly it's also the case of *El Quijote*. In that, we don't think of each chapter, even less of each page. Rather, what remains of the book once the volume is shut. There is something that remains, and that is an image, and that image is something that one clearly remembers.

FERRARI. And which the volume can disregard.

BORGES. And which can be disregarded, yes.

6

The Book of Sand

●

OSVALDO FERRARI. In relation to the books you published in recent years, Borges, you frequently repeated your predilection for *The Book of Sand*.

JORGE LUIS BORGES. Yes, I think of all my books it's the most easy reading, and to be legible is a virtue. There are big books that don't have it and don't seek it. Joyce's work, for example, and *La guerra gaucha* by Lugones . . . they were not written to be read but to be admired, analysed, commented on. But now I cherish that modest ambition: to be legible. And although my stories are complex—since there's nothing in the world that isn't—given that the world is inexplicable, I try to make what I write seem simple, and I take a fundamental precaution: to avoid words that may suggest to the reader that he consult a dictionary. And in this, clearly, I oppose myself to all our present linguistic habits. For example, 'methodology' instead of 'method', 'busqueda' instead of 'busca', 'thematic' instead of 'theme'. Currently, the use of longer words is looked for, but not by me. I try to use simple words, and, moreover, I want to tell the story in a way that makes the reader ask himself: And now what? It seems to me that's important. One has to think of a text that maybe could be called very interesting. I was rereading with my sister the stories about Sherlock Holmes by Conan Doyle. The arguments are poor, the phrases ingenious, they are not excessive, but one is continually interested in the plot—the solutions are weak but the enigmas, the little enigmas are interesting. It seems to me that is enough for a story. Now, if I had to choose a book among mine—I don't do it since there are no books of mine in this house—I would choose *The Book of Sand*. But they've said to me *Doctor Brodie's Report* is superior. The truth is I don't know very well to which volume each of the stories belongs. They have told me 'El Congreso' is my best story and I think that is in *Doctor Brodie's Report*.

FERRARI. No, it's in *The Book of Sand*.

BORGES. Then, my predilection for *The Book of Sand* . . .

FERRARI. Is confirmed.

BORGES. Yes, it is confirmed. And I think that 'The Book of Sand' is a lovely story.

FERRARI. But you never speak of that story. It is the last in the book and, for me, very important.

BORGES. I don't know if it's important, because 'The Book of Sand' is 'El Aleph', 'El Zahir', 'Funes el memorioso' more or less in fancy dress. In other words, is the idea of something that seems beautiful and that then later is terrible.

FERRARI. In that line of correspondences I could say that the first story in the book 'El Otro' links naturally with your story 'Borges y yo'.

BORGES. Yes, but I believe that 'Borges y yo' came out better, eh? For a start, it's very brief, it has that merit. Now, as for the other stories, I don't know which is best.

FERRARI. 'Avelino Arredondo' is very lovely.

BORGES. Yes, but 'Avelino Arredondo' was given me . . . by the history of the República Oriental (Uruguay), since the action occurred but is not repeated. Let's say, a terrorist assassinates the president. Then he immediately gives himself up to the police and assumes all responsibility. An uncle of mine, Luis Melian Lafinur, defended him and was able to tell me many things about Avelino Arredondo. But when I wrote the story, Luis Melian Lafinur had already died. And he had been his defender. I think they gave him two years in prison since everyone admired Arredondo—not for the action of having assassinated Iriarte Borda but for the action of assuming all responsibility, something that is not too frequent. I think there are accused persons now that think less of assuming responsibility than in good defending lawyers, aren't there? In the justice that took place in Nuremberg, it also occurred. Then I, to remedy in some way those accused, I invented a perfect Nazi, a man to whom it seemed that it was fine that they were inexorable with him since he had been inexorable with others, and I wrote that story 'Deutsche Requiem' which many interpreted as my adhesion to Hitler's cause. No, it's not that. I tried to imagine a Nazi who was really one, a Nazi who was ruthless, not only with others—which is easy—but ruthless with himself and who accepted that lot as just. It seems that in reality that is not given, eh? It seems that people tend rather to take pity on themselves and not on others. The classic example would be Martín Fierro, a sentimental ruffian who continually took pity on himself and who took not the slightest pity on others. But that seems pretty common.

FERRARI. If, Borges, it seems right to you, I'd like to read fragments of the story 'Avelino Arredondo' so that we may recall it together.

BORGES. Well, why not? You've got the text? Because in this house there are no books of mine.

FERRARI (*laughs*). I've got it.

BORGES. Then it's fine.

FERRARI. We recall, then, he retires from public life so as not, in secret, to compromise others in the plan that is going to be put into practise.

BORGES. Well, I had to invent all the circumstances, because I didn't know where he'd hidden himself. Perhaps he went to the countryside. But I knew nothing about that. I knew he stopped seeing his girl-friend, his friends, so as not to compromise anyone. Nor did he read the daily papers, so that they could not think that the dailies' continuous attacks on the president had influenced him. In other words, he was an individual. So, let's see.

FERRARI. You say, for example: 'He changed to a room in the back which gave onto the earth patio. The measure was useless but it helped him to initiate that reclusion that his will imposed on himself. From the narrow iron bed in which he was recovering his habit of having siestas he was looking with some sadness at an empty shelf. He had sold all his books, including those of an introduction to law. There remained no more than a bible that he had never read and that didn't conclude. He studied it page by page, sometimes with interest, sometimes with boredom, and he imposed on himself the duty of learning by heart some chapter from Exodus and the end of Ecclesiastes. He did not try to understand what he was reading. He was a free thinker . . . '

BORGES. It's verisimilar. It's all verisimilar, it seems to me.

FERRARI. It is. You said you were a free thinker.

BORGES. Yes, in that time they used that phrase, free thinker. Now, it's not used, is it? Or is it? Free thinker in English, in French it's *esprit fort* which is like a homage to the free thinkers, *espíritu fuerte* in Spanish. It means, or wanted to mean, an atheist in French. In the eighteenth century, it was used when one didn't allow oneself to be subjugated to various authorities.

FERRARI. 'He was a free thinker, but he didn't let a single night pass, without repeating the Our Father, which he'd promised his mother in Montevideo . . . '

BORGES. Good, that characteristic is autobiographical: I promised my mother to repeat the 'Our Father' and I did it every night. Which is to say that I, at that time, intervened in the imaginary destiny of Avelino Arredondo (*laughs*).

FERRARI. That, Borges, constitutes an unexpected revelation (*laughs*).

BORGES. A modest revelation.

FERRARI. 'To fail that promise could have brought him bad luck.'

BORGES. Ah, that's good, the superstitious side also. All that makes Avelino Arredondo more or less conceivable.

FERRARI. Clearly, and it goes on gradually introducing us to the facts.

BORGES. I had to invent circumstantial features since the style of our time demands it.

FERRARI. 'He knew his objective was the morning of the 25th of August. He knew the precise number of days he had to surmount. Once the objective was achieved, time would cease, or better said, nothing important could happen afterwards . . . '

BORGES. When one waits something that always occurs—for example, when I'm in Europe, I think: 'When I return to Buenos Aires.' And now I think: 'When I am in Italy, or when I am in Japan . . . ', as if nothing was going to happen afterwards. Or when one is waiting . . . well, a man who is waiting for a woman, he thinks thus also: 'The important thing is that she arrives.' (*Both laugh*) After that: What does it matter?

FERRARI. 'He waited for the date as whoever awaits happiness and a liberation. He had stopped his watch so as not to be always looking at it, but every night, hearing the twelve dark peals, he tore a sheet from the calendar and thought, one day less . . . '

BORGES. That was done by a friend who was a doctor in La Pampa and who knew that he had to be a certain number of days in a place—he tore the leaf of the almanac. That is to say, I don't invent anything (*laughs*), that circumstances give me everything, and what else can a man do?

FERRARI (*laughs*). But the circumstances have given him very special things In this case. 'At the beginning . . .'

BORGES. I'm listening with great curiosity. I don't know what's going to happen, for it's now so many years since I wrote that story . . .

FERRARI. We're reaching the decisive moment: 'At the beginning he wanted to construe a routine. To drink maté, to smoke the black cigarettes he carried, to read and revise a certain quota of pages, to try to talk to Clementina when she brings him lunch on a tray, to repeat and to adorn a certain option before turning off the light. To talk to Clementina, a woman already old, because her memory had remained in the country and the daily life of the country. He also benefits from a chess board on which he played messy games which didn't turn out right. He lacked a tower which he used to substitute with a ball and a copper coin . . . '

BORGES. Good, that about the bullet is good, because in some moments he prepares the final shot.

FERRARI. Yes.

BORGES. The *vintén*, good, local Uruguayan colour. In Uruguay, they talk of *vintenes*, something they don't speak of here, do they?

FERRARI. We're going to have to explain, Borges, where we localize that bullet and at whom it was directed.

BORGES. That bullet was destined towards the president of the republic whom it was going to assassinate.

FERRARI. The president of the Oriental Republic of Uruguay.

BORGES. Yes, Iriarte Borda. No, what's strange is all that is unknown here, so many people think I have invented that story. But it's an episode that nobody ignores in Uruguay, except a person who has forgotten it. I don't remember the date it happened . . . but it has to be around the first decade of the twentieth century.

7

Blaise Pascal

●

OSVALDO FERRARI. Although in your case, Borges, I often think that your chief preoccupation has been time, in the case of Pascal, it's been space, concretely.

JORGE LUIS BORGES. Yes, one feels vertigo, faced with infinite space. Now, curiously, if you re-read *De Rerum Natura* by Lucretius, he was captivated by the idea of infinite space.

FERRARI. Of an infinite universe.

BORGES. Of an infinite universe, yes, he felt a kind of vertigo but a pleasant vertigo. And I once observed that Spengler said that for the Greeks, and consequently for the Romans, their disciples, the world is made by a series of volumes in space. And then comes Faustian culture which delights in the idea of infinite time and infinite space. But Lucretius, a long time before Faustian culture, had already been captivated by that idea which later terrified Pascal.

FERRARI. Of course.

BORGES. Curiously. I may say, a book such as *De Rerum Natura* came to be earlier than the *Pensée* of Pascal, not only chronologically but in mentality. Now the idea of infinite space or time does not terrify us. Or, in every case our imaginations accept it.

FERRARI. The ideas of Copérnicus and Galileo were also before Pascal.

BORGES. Yes, and I think that Cicero was delighted with the idea of space peopled by worlds which would be spherical like ours, and some of them repeated. I believe he thought while he writes these lines, another Cicero, on another planet, is writing the same, which would anticipate the idea of what Nietzsche would much later call 'the eternal return' but not only in time—also in space. An infinite space, with all possible or contemporary worlds. That is . . . in the treatise *Of the Nature of the Gods* of Cicero, yes, *De Natura Orum* on some page, is that. Of course it has to come from some Greek, I don't believe that Cicero invented it, do you? In some Greek, it will have been read.

FERRARI. Everything comes from the Greeks.

BORGES. I believe so. Cicero was a good reader of the Greeks.

FERRARI. Yes, precisely, and the *Humanities*. But Pascal's terror was not only the immensity of space but also the minimum of us. That is to say, he saw that we almost don't exist in that immensity.

BORGES. Yes, he felt that vertigo. On the other hand, Lucretius was convinced by that idea.

FERRARI. Pascal's phrase is: 'The infinite immensity of space which I ignore and which ignores me'—which you record in your essay.

BORGES. I believe that has been judged by Valéry, because Valéry says that for many thinkers previous, contemporary and after Pascal, well, the starry vault has not given them that impression. On the contrary, they have seen an order in it. They have not felt terror but a certain felicity on seeing that those infinite stars are ordered and obey laws and in some way are a proof of the existence of God.

FERRARI. That space is cosmic.

BORGES. That space is cosmic, yes, that it is cosmic and not chaotic.

FERRARI. The other phenomenon that seems to have produced another form of vertigo in Pascal, although a more secret vertigo, is that of the incarnation and the crucifixion of Christ. This is appreciated, above all, in his last books: that the idea of incarnation and divinity produced in him a kind of interior scandal.

BORGES. Well, the agnostics, or an agnostic sect, said that Christ had not been crucified, that he who was crucified was a ghost because a god could not suffer, well, torments and pain.

FERRARI. That a god cannot become incarnate.

BORGES. He cannot become incarnate: one supposes, then, that Christ was an apparition, a kind of divine ghost. That is to say, they deny that Christ had taken corporal shape. And the idea of a god eating, directing, sweating—all that, seems so hard . . . one would have to suppose that constituted a sacrifice greater than that of being crucified, the act of humbling oneself to a human body. That divinity, the creator of all the universe, encloses itself in a human body, with the limitations and . . . the small humiliations of a material body . . .

FERRARI. Now, I'm not sure . . . I recall that Spinoza identified God with nature . . .

BORGES. Yes, he says: *God serves nature.* Good, but that is the idea of pantheism, the idea that all is God.

FERRARI. All is God.

BORGES. All is divine, but that divinity, well, one could suppose that in minerals it is dead, that in plants it is sleeping, that in animals it's always beginning to dream, and that in man, man would come to be the conscience of all that, he would come to be *it*. Man, or the human mind which conceives time, something that other genres, or other species, don't conceive.

FERRARI. Exactly. But in the case of Pascal it would be different from that of Spinoza. Pascal speaks of the universe, but not as if the universe or nature were God.

BORGES. Ah no, it's understood that they are God's work, eh? How strange. Blake spoke of the world with much disdain, calleing it 'the vegetable world', that is, the world as a kind of vegetable, didn't he? And he said, well, he said it in full romantic epoch, that the spectacle of natural things was something that did not arouse him. But then, he said he saw them in another way. For example, if he saw the dawn, he did not see it as a luminous disc that arose—no, he saw all that as a divinity, surrounded by angels (*laughs*). He saw natural things as if they were already myths. Let's say, he saw the sun—but what he saw was, in some way Apollo. Except he called it another divinity in his private mythology.

FERRARI. Greece would be present there too.

BORGES. Greece would be present there too. It seems Greece is always present.

FERRARI. It's ubiquitous.

BORGES. I recall a pun of, damn, I'm sorry to say, Alfonso Reyes. But, well, he said it in passing whereas now I'm overdoing it: 'To So-and-So, full of grace', and then, comma or in parenthesis, 'full of Greece' (*laughs*). That we can forgive him—those lines he wrote, doubtless, with a smile, didn't he?

FERRARI. With a smile, but deep down there is praise there.

BORGES. Yes, there is praise as well, yes, of course. One would have thought, or one thinks, when he read that line, that the fact that 'Greece' and 'grace' are alike isn't chance. They were predestined, in some way, those two words; 'full of grace', 'full of Greece' and perhaps in a melodious paragraph, for a melodious page, that line passes and is forgiven or admitted, isn't that so?

FERRARI. Without any doubt.

BORGES. On the other hand, I, taking it out of context, am betraying my master and a dear friend who has died: Alfonso Reyes. So that we can forget that joke, which was only a joke, since without doubt he wrote it on a page while smiling.

FERRARI. A final comment, Borges, that you make in your essay about Pascal.

BORGES. I'd like to recall that essay—I wrote it so long ago that all I remember is the title, and perhaps the colour of the cover of the book. How sad that all that remains of a book are some physical circumstances such as those, don't you think?

FERRARI. In this case they are a given.

BORGES. All that remains is that green memory (*both laugh*), to give it the name of the journal which Rodolfo Wilcock got out, *Verde Memoria*, yes.

FERRARI. I refer, then, to that sphere which was the centre of the universe and which had no circumference, it began being a natural idea, and finally Pascal spoke of it as an appalling sphere.

BORGES. He wanted to say that the universe seemed terrible to him. It's that, in fact, isn't it? Although Chesterton thought that he should thank everything, but taking account that they were terrible. He said that he was going to die and that he will not have thanked God for all the grass. In other words, something so simple, such as grass, no?

FERRARI. Every single thing. Pascal also, I think, had a religious attitude towards gratitude. Nevertheless, terror continued in him up to the end.

BORGES. Yes, that is the memory I have of Pascal.

8

The Imitative Country

●

OSVALDO FERRARI. Recently, Borges, you have demonstrated a particular preoccupation with teaching, especially in the Faculty of Philosophy and Letters. But I know that this preoccupation also touches other faculties and universities.

JORGE LUIS BORGES. Yes, I was in the illustrious University of Córdoba where among others, Dr Francia was educated. Although I came back with, let's say, a rather disagreeable impression. They invited me to attend, a class, but the name alarmed me—Dynamic Psychology. Well, now, my father was professor of Psychology in Living Tongues, and I have always been interested in psychology. And I believed that psychology was the study of human conscience, that psychology was what they had studied. And let's say, the scholastics, William James, Spiller . . . I believed that they dealt with studying a conscience, the habit or mechanisms of conscience, and then such rare things as dreams, sleep, memory, forgetfulness, the will. I believed that such was the field of psychology.

FERRARI. Yes.

BORGES. I also remembered Bergson, naturally. But then I attended that class. Perhaps the name had alarmed me: Dynamic Psychology. The professor, whose name I don't wish to remember, and what's more I've forgotten it, began to trace with chalk on the blackboard the words 'Prologue Class', a not-very-happy compound word but which the students, who were, I don't know, some hundred strong, had to copy. That class lasted half an hour: Dynamic Psychology. And I realized that it had nothing to do with either psychology or dynamism, since it consisted of a series of, well, confusions based on the etymology of words.

Now, I'm very interested in etymology, as you know, above all because one sees that very different concepts have the same root. For example, I recently found out that 'kleptomaniac' and 'clepsydra' had the same origin. They are not at all alike but, in the first case, kleptomaniac, well, is a thief, isn't it? That is, he steals, he takes money or whatever. And the clepsydra takes water. Or what we have observed on other occasions: that the terrible word 'nausea' that no writer dares to use has a beautiful origin in the word 'nave'. From 'nave', perhaps pronounced 'navis', come 'naval', 'nautical' and 'nausea', because one feels nausea on deck. The fact of seeing that very distinct words have the same root has always amused me.

But the theme of Dynamic Psychology was the contrary: it tried to demonstrate that the two words were synonyms because they had the same root. Then they took the words 'crear' (to create) and 'creer' (to believe)—I don't know if they have the same root—at any rate, it seems to me absurd to reach the conclusion that both are synonyms.

The argument was that if one believes, one creates . . . well, one believes in what has been created. Now, that would be a kind of play on words, a pun, a *greguería*. And six or seven examples are given, no less precious but happily more forgettable than those I've just mentioned, and the students had to note those games and that, it is supposed, that is a subject. That is studied and then they take an exam on that subject   although now I think examinations almost don't exist, since you are urged to enter university without previous exams, there are group exams in which one student answers for others. Moreover, the professors are a little terrorized by the students, and it's a terrible fact that universities, instead of teaching, dedicate themselves to encouraging arbitrariness or illusory sciences, such as Dynamic Psychology. I hope that things proceed better in other parts.

FERRARI. You observed that in Córdoba?

BORGES. Yes, I observed it in Córdoba. It seemed very strange to me because I had the impression that everything is ordered thus, that what one is dealing with is simply . . . well, perhaps the professors are able to exhibit certain vanities, don't you think? In any case, they can surprise students. It's a pity the university is not taken advantage of for study, but is used for mere occurrences. I think that here also the study of literature, for example, seems to disregard completely the taste for aesthetic fact.

FERRARI. You say here in Buenos Aires?

BORGES. Yes, and perhaps also in a good part of the world, yes, that is disregarded and mere games are looked for. I fear psychology was replaced by psychoanalysis, but not simply by a series of word games and etymologies.

FERRARI. In which the will of the student is needed to accept the proposal, let's say.

BORGES. Yes, but the students are very docile . . . That isn't difficult, I mean, those trivialities are learned and are learned without great effort, isn't it so?

FERRARI. They are memorized, in any case.

BORGES. They are memorized, in any case. Well, with luck one can get to forget them later. (*Laughs*) If one is lucky, one can forget all that has been memorized for the exam.

FERRARI. After having passed, let's say.

BORGES. Yes, after having passed, one can forget everything, nothing is lost. Is it? But it is very sad, because this country is declining—we all know that—and it is a pity the declination be not only ethically and economically but also intellectually. And that is what is promoted, possibly for political reasons, isn't that so? A criterion of committee is being shuffled. In Córdoba, I was told the number of students there were—an exorbitant figure!

FERRARI. What was it?

BORGES. I don't remember, but I know it was tens of thousands. And I don't know if the professors can cope with that quantity. They would have to try to restrict the number of students in order to study, really. But it seems that statistics are very important in this epoch, aren't they? It seems that statistics are in fashion. Well, I once defined democracy as the abuse of statistics, and if the universities are going to follow the same path, it follows that the important thing is not that someone learns but that there should be many students. And then we have in this country a tendency towards euphemisms, which can, well, enlarge things. For example, I know university cities, among others some in the United States, that really are cities—the lecture halls are there, and the students and the professors live there. Here, they have joined two faculties in some or other quarter and that they call a university city, but it's not a university city because nobody lives there. It seems that words suffice.

FERRARI. Yes, meanings are abused.

BORGES. For example, the fact that we suffer from eighty-two generals . . . maybe it would have been more important if there had been one. Perhaps it would be too much to demand one. On the other hand, eighty-two can be eighty-two incompetents, eighty-two enthusiasts, eighty-two in fancy dress, eighty-two in uniform.

FERRARI. That reminds me of a phrase of yours referring to the country: a military man is possibly a civilian in uniform.

BORGES. Yes, and I believe you said to me that many civilians are essentially military officers without a uniform.

FERRARI. Yes, effectively.

BORGES. Not in their strategic attitude but, yes, in the love of the arbitrary, the violence. We could say they don't know how to win a battle, but to arrest a citizen—that, yes.

FERRARI. Then, I see that throughout this year—it had already become manifest in the previous year—the preoccupation with what is happening in our universities persists.

BORGES. Well, it's natural that it be so. I was professor of English literature in the Faculty of Philosophy and Letters for twenty years. I did not teach English literature—that I ignored—but the love—I don't say of the whole of literature, because that would be absurd—but, yes, of certain writers and certain books. I believe not to have failed in that intention.

So that what is happening there pains me. It's true I'm an emeritus professor and a consultant, but they've never consulted me about anything and I don't know what that means. I asked José Luis Romero—they nominated the two of us as emeritus professors or consultants—what does this mean? Well, he said to me, the truth is I haven't the slightest idea but I suppose the intention is friendly. Because if it isn't a mere phonetic gift, what is it? They add or they give those two epithets to one.

FERRARI. And after having manifested your preoccupation, have you still not been consulted in recent times?

BORGES. No, above all having manifested, it's not convenient to consult me, is it? (*Laughs*) I'm not going to approve any of the bagatelles that are inflicted, that are bestowed rather, or that are offered to lazy students.

FERRARI. Perhaps one of the things that most costs Argentineans in this epoch is to be conscious and to maintain a consciousness open to what occurs. In that sense, your attitude seems to me important, because although it be uncomfortable, it is directed at consciousness.

BORGES. But it is that for me, it's not only uncomfortable but also sad.

FERRARI. For that, the duty of consciousness.

BORGES. Yes, what I find so astonishing is that supposed subject, whose name I gave you: Dynamic Psychology but which has nothing to do with dynamics or psychology.

FERRARI. The Greek is present (*laughs*).

BORGES (*laughs*). Yes, present, the Greek, it's true. I don't know where they have got that from, I don't believe it's a Cordobesque invention, like 'university reform', I think not. Doubtless it's taught in another part of the world, no? We have, above all, an imitative country.

9

St Thomas and the Talmud

●

OSVALDO FERRARI. It sometimes interests me, Borges, to return to that book you compiled with Adolfo Bioy Casares and which appeared very like a title of a book by Blake. I speak of the *Book of Heaven and Hell*.

JORGE LUIS BORGES. Of course, yes, Blake's book is *The Weddings* . . .

FERRARI. *Matrimony.*

BORGES. Oh, *Matrimony of Heaven and Hell, Marriage of Heaven and Hell,* yes.

FERRARI. Now, in the *Book of Heaven and Hell* . . .

BORGES. Doubtless, you have to have texts by Blake, don't you?

FERRARI. Yes, I confirm that. But the one that interests me is a fragment of St Thomas Aquinas called 'Resurrection of the Flesh'.

BORGES. No, I don't think it's St Thomas, I believe it's Origen. No, what I remember is that it's a passage by Origen. Origen says that the sphere is a perfect form. Perfect means that all the points of the surface are equidistant from the centre. When the resurrection of the flesh occurs, people, us let's say, we are going to resuscitate in spherical form and enter heaven rolling. Isn't that the passage? Possibly, it's another, no?

FERRARI. I think it doesn't seem so similar, but it would be marvellous if it were that. He says: 'Only what is necessary for the reality of nature will resuscitate.' That is the first phrase, 'All I have said about the integrity of men after the resurrection must refer to what belongs to the reality of human nature, because what doesn't belong to the truth of human nature will not be restored to resuscitated men.'

BORGES. That means to say resuscitated persons without their sins. That means, for example, I will come back from the dead not being blind, doesn't it? Or that a person, a person with leprosy, will come back from the dead with a healthy body, isn't that so?

FERRARI. He explains it in that way.

BORGES. Or that those who resuscitate will be just.

FERRARI. It's possible.

BORGES. No, I don't think so, because if some are condemned to hell . . . I don't know what explanation that may have. Moreover, 'the reality of human nature' is a vague term that can signify nothing or everything.

FERRARI. He says: 'Anyway it would be necessary for all men to be of extraordinary magnitude, if all the foods converted into flesh and blood were resuscitated.' Even the explanation is strange.

BORGES. It means to say that when a person resuscitates, he will resuscitate with all the loaves he has eaten, doesn't it? Well, it will be augmented by the volume of all the glasses of water that have been taken, isn't that so? Because if it's not that, it's not anything.

FERRARI. Good, let's proceed, and with luck it might be explained.

BORGES. I already feel a great curiosity. It seems, doesn't it, that all the explanations are nonsense.

FERRARI (*laughs*). Certainly. 'It is so, that they only pay attention to the truth of each nature according to its kind. Then the parts of the men who are considered according to his species and his form are found fully integrated in the resuscitated men, like the organic parts and the similar parts, like flesh, nerves and all the things of this genre that engage in the composition of the organs.'

BORGES. That means that nobody will come back as a pygmy or as a giant, that all will be resuscitated in, I don't know, in the same stature, isn't that what is meant?

FERRARI. Let's go on—with luck every thing will be cleared up.

BORGES. Let's go on, with luck everything will be cleared up or we'll reach what Valéry believed very difficult—a perfect chaos, a perfect disorder (*laughs*), because already now we are losing ourselves in the woods.

FERRARI. 'Not all the matter that there may have been in these parts during their natural state will be restored, but only that which was sufficient for the integrity of the species of these parts.'

BORGES. That we won't resuscitate with all the sardines we've eaten, for example.

FERRARI (*laughs*). Foreseeably no, it's increasingly difficult.

BORGES. But I don't know if anyone has thought of that possibility.

FERRARI. It's very strange, because he adds: 'Nevertheless, the man will not stop being numerically the same in his integrity, even when materially he does not resuscitate all that materially there may have been in him. In effect, it's evident that man in this life is numerically the same from the beginning to the end.'

BORGES. Good, the mystery is in the adverb 'numerically'. What does numerically mean? Does it mean quantitatively or not?

FERRARI. It's obvious, it's the only possible explanation, by quantity.

BORGES. One thing that has to be known is this: The day of the last judgement, an ancient is going to resuscitate as an ancient, or not? Resuscitate at what is supposed to be the perfect age, that is to say, at thirty-three or thirty-five. These are the two possibilities: thirty-three of course would be the age at which Christ is crucified and when Adam is born. And thirty-five would be following Dante in his most famous verse, 'Nel mezzo del camin di nostra vita'. That is, if the way of life is seventy years, 'Nel mezzo del camin' means thirty-five, Moreover, he explains that in 'La vita nuova'.

FERRARI. I'm going, then, to the last paragraph.

BORGES. Let's see, let's see, let's see if we reach an appreciation or we arrive at what Milton called: 'Confused words confounded' (*laughs*).

FERRARI (*laughs*). 'However, what is materially in him under the species of the parts, does not remain the same, but is subject to loss or increment, in the way that fire keeps the same by the addition of wood, the more it is consumed. Man is entire when the species is preserved and the convenient quantity of the species.'

BORGES. I don't know if you're feeling a little lost. I really . . .

FERRARI. I think that for the first time, Borges, we are almost completely lost. This has been the labyrinth of St Thomas.

BORGES. Yes, and what's extraordinary is that this has not been done in order to be labyrinthine but in order to be explicative.

FERRARI. Exactly.

BORGES. All this is an explication, and that explication is precisely the mysterious, isn't it? I recall a verse of Byron speaking of Coleridge, and he says that Coleridge is 'explaining metaphysics to the nation'. And he adds: 'Would that he would explain his explanation'. I think that can be applied not only to Coleridge but also to St Thomas, can't it? Would that he would explain his explanation, since his explanation seems more nebulous than whatever enigma, than whatever problem he may be discussing.

FERRARI. It's that, differently from St Augustine, St Thomas, in the line of Aristotle, always directs himself exclusively to reason, and that is what makes things more difficult—because we cannot imagine, we can only reason.

BORGES. In this case, I'm not sure of being able to reason, because I followed that argument and I don't understand it. Now clearly there is that phrase so mysterious, how it is: the reality of nature or the nature of reality, I don't know which of the two it is, or neither of the two.

FERRARI. 'It will only resuscitate what is necessary for the reality of nature.'

BORGES. Which means?

FERRARI. It's confusing. Perhaps Chesterton, who did the portrait of St Thomas Aquinas . . .

BORGES. He said that for St Francis of Assisi, an outline was enough. But in the case of St Thomas, a plan was necessary. We should need that grand plan to see if it helps us. Yes, in St Thomas' case we are dealing with a map.

FERRARI. Surely, now, in regard to the portrait of St Thomas that Chesterton did, you'll recall that it was an excellent portrait.

BORGES. Yes it was excellent, but I don't think it refers to this passage. I think that would have defeated Chesterton. No, he would have invented a very ingenious explanation. More ingenious than the text explained, and so ingenious that we would have accepted it, wouldn't we? I don't believe this can be explained. Are you sure that this appears in the book?

FERRARI. It appears.

BORGES. We shall have placed it like a museum piece, without doubt, like a diversion, something for . . . well, not to annoy but to make the reader uneasy, let's say.

FERRARI. A commentator on Chesterton's book about St Thomas says, maybe exaggerating things, that St Thomas has done well to wait seven centuries to entrust his portrait to Chesterton.

BORGES. That means to say that the portrait is more acceptable . . . than the *Suma Teológica*, doesn't it? And that it costs nothing to believe (*laughs*).

FERRARI. It's an interpretation Huxley gives.

BORGES. Let's see . . .

FERRARI. That says that towards the end of his life, St Thomas felt that everything he had written . . . the words are literally: 'That all I have written before seemed so much straw.' Much matter, so, almost insignificant, perhaps because he had reached the contemplative state.

BORGES. And, but the fact that he later reaches the contemplative state, doesn't that serve to explain this previous rough draft—doesn't it?

FERRARI. You continue to worry about the resurrection of the flesh which is not explained in this case.

BORGES. Of course, it's less picturesque than that by Origen, because the idea that persons will resuscitate in the shape of spheres . . . did not say anything about the size of the spheres. I don't know if they'll all be equal, perhaps not, eh? Well, it's clear that Origen's is a play of words. The fact that a sphere may be a perfect form does not mean that a sphere would be more pleasant for the sight than a column, or an equestrian statue of Colleone or of Gattamelata. Simply the most perfect from that point of view—the fact that each point of the surface is equidistant from the centre, but not the most perfect aesthetically. If a sculptor dedicates himself only to make spheres, I don't think he'd have much success, do you? Well, this occurs with that strange theory of cubism: the idea that all shape can be reduced to cubes. Now, I don't know why they may be reduced to cubes, and not, let's say, to pyramids, or cones, or cylinders. One would have to study the theory of cubism, if there was a theory of cubism, something that we'll never know, will we? Above all, if we dedicate ourselves to study that theme.

FERRARI. In order to compensate you, Borges, for this attempt, perhaps frustrated, that we have done with the text of St Thomas.

BORGES. No, but what has failed is St Thomas (*both laugh*). He is the saint, not us. We aren't saints and we haven't failed.

FERRARI. We haven't failed.

BORGES. Well, failed in the attempt to understand this.

FERRARI. There is another text in the *Book of Heaven and Hell* . . .

BORGES. Good, let's see, we hope that it be less . . .

FERRARI. That is more explicit, more concrete . . .

BORGES. Less shadowy and less mysterious than this.

FERRARI. It's in the Talmud and says: 'Heaven for the Jews'. 'The Garden of Eden is sixty times better than Egypt. It is situated in the seventh sphere of the firmament.' We spoke before about spheres, now we have a concrete sphere.

BORGES. Yes.

FERRARI. 'Through its two doors enter sixty myriads of angels with faces brilliant as the firmament.'

BORGES. Yes, I believe that everything is so big that it's inconceivable, isn't it? It seems that if one speaks of two angels, one can believe in them, but if one speaks of thousands of angels, the figure already exceeds the imagination's possibilities. The bigger, the more indefinite.

FERRARI. However, it becomes more concrete.

BORGES. Let's see.

FERRARI. 'When a just man reaches Eden, the angels undress him, they adorn his head with two crowns, one of gold and the other with precious stones; they put into his hands eight myrtle sticks, dancing around him, they don't cease to sing with pleasant tone: "Eat your bread and rejoice." '

BORGES. Well I don't know if it will be easy to eat the bread if eight sticks obstruct, don't you think? It's hard to imagine this scene.

FERRARI (*laughs*). In you, Borges.

BORGES. Happily, almost no painter has attempted it, I don't think so. It would be very difficult to draw that uncomfortable thing justly. Rejoice, fine, eating a loaf which has not been previously mentioned either. One does that *ex nihilo*, out of nothing.

FERRARI. It often catches my attention, Borges, the fact that you seem to unite two capacities. The manner of thinking by strict reasoning of St Thomas, and the other, the Augustinian or Platonic, the mythical.

BORGES. Well, what you've just read me, I don't know to what mode it conforms. It seems more mythical but it's not particularly pleasant, is it? It seems a person who tries to imagine something and who fails. And he covers large quantities.

FERRARI. I regret this double failure of today, Borges, but . . .

BORGES. But it's not ours, it's the theologians.

10

Liberalism and Nationalism

●

OSVALDO FERRARI. For some of my generation, Borges, it becomes curious and even incomprehensible, that perpetual disagreement between nationalists and liberals about tradition or lack of tradition in Argentinean literature and culture.

JORGE LUIS BORGES. The same thing happens to me. Of course, one is talking about a search for identity, but better not find it in my opinion. Because we are, well, as I've said more than once, let's say, occidentals and Europeans in exile, in a happy exile. Now, curiously, the nationalists insist on denying the differential characteristic of this country, which is strong immigration. For all America—without excluding the North—the Argentinean differential characteristic is that, and it is precisely what the nationalists deny. They want us to be Spanish and Indian, which is what all the other countries of South America are. How strange that they should deny our most evident differential characteristic. But that's what they do: the nationalists don't insist that this is a country of immigration, they admit only the Spanish—they insist that the indigenous hardly exist here. They are by nature illogical.

FERRARI. But the strangest would seem to be up to what point this problem has divided the different generations of this country.

BORGES. I suppose that for the men of the eighties, the idea of immigration was a valuable idea. In other periods, it was seen as a danger.

FERRARI. As a danger for identity, are you saying?

BORGES. Yes, I understand that it is, and it is understood that all our ills proceed from immigration. But no, our ills, well, they follow from the War of Independence, and we have in continuation anarchy, *caudillos* (leaders), all this was before immigration. I recall that during the dictatorship of Perón, there were people who said that this was due to the immigrants. And I had to show them, well, that Perónism was very strong in the interior where there is less immigration. And recently it was that in Tucumán which came to be the place where that type was most venerated by them, the mixture of Spanish and Indian, that's where there was, let's say, war.

FERRARI. In the plane of literature it has probably been Lugones who, from that idea that he proposed in *El Payador*, perhaps generated the polemic.

BORGES. Nevertheless, Lugones is inconceivable without French literature. Moreover he professed the cult of Dante.

FERRARI. Yes, but at the proposing of *Martín Fierro* . . .

BORGES. But that corresponds to an idea which for me is superstitious, that each country must have a holy book. Then to him it occurs, this book, which is, let's say, this Koran or that Bible, it could be *Martín Fierro*. How strange! I have heard people who, while conversing with foreign men of letters, have given them a copy of *Martín Fierro* and who have said: 'It's our Bible.' Which seems very bizarre doesn't it? Nevertheless, it is accepted . . .

FERRARI. But that implies that one had to write in the gauchoesque tradition? That to write in Argentina implied prolonging that tradition?

BORGES. No. I don't think so, I think that it supposed that, with *Martín Fierro*, one had reached the apex. No I don't believe that they thought to continue the tradition. That was a 'sacred book'—up to what point could it be imitated without blasphemy? I don't think that writers who tried analogous themes considered themselves heirs to that tradition. On the contrary, when *Don Segundo Sombra* appeared it was sponsored by Lugones. An article by Jorge Alimano came out in the journal *Sur*, and in that article he praised the book and said: We always suspect that Martín Fierro did not correspond to the gaucho and now we have proof (the testimony of *Don Segundo Sombra* where the gaucho is demonstrated as a tranquil man, a man of peace and not necessarily a deserter and a fugitive). Güiraldes got to tell me once also that Don Segundo Sombra was more representative of the gaucho than Martín Fierro. Of course, since the majority of countrymen were not gauchos on the run.

FERRARI. Yes, clearly, in that more than half a century at least, between the two types of gaucho.

BORGES. But yes, yes of course. And I don't know that the type of gaucho was still around when Güiraldes published *Don Segundo Sombra*, I believe not. I believe that *Don Segundo Sombra* must be read, let's say, from Ricardo's childhood on the ranch. Just as the Palermo that Carriego describes in *Alma del suburbio* was already an anachronism when he published the book . . . well, there will have been cases of violence before, among the *cuchilleros*, but I don't recall any violence in Palermo. But it's that everything was calmer then, not only in Palermo, wasn't it?

FERRARI. Possibly, it was written on the basis of previous myths.

BORGES. Yes, I think so. And in the case of Carriego, he could have thought in that tradition of courage, which had to have been stronger in Entre Ríos than in Buenos Aires.

FERRARI. Also you have said that Ricardo Reyes has given an idea of the origin of gauchoesque poetry which could have caused confusion.

BORGES. Clearly, since when he speaks of gauchoesque poetry he calls them *payador* (singer) and none of them was a *payador*, as far as I know. Well, perhaps Ascasubi was, but there is no constancy either. No, I think not. I think it's evident that gauchoesque poetry had its origin in the cities.

FERRARI. Is it Buenos Aires which invented the gaucho and the pampas?

BORGES. I think so, but they are good inventions. Buenos Aires must not be reproached for that. On the contrary, it should be thanked.

FERRARI. In relation to all this, I think you have shown that what has been expressed in one manner or another by the Argentinean writer are the profound tendencies of the Argentinean man. For example, you have quoted verses by Banchs in which he warns of a type of reticence or of self-reserve of the man of here.

BORGES. Yes, and precisely when he is not looking for local colour, in those verses in which he speaks of nightingales and rooftops, no? 'The sun on the rooftops / and in the windows shines. Nightingales mean they are in love.' Clearly, he is speaking of nightingales and rooftops instead of flat roofs and larks, for example.

FERRARI. Although the nightingales and the rooftops are foreigners, the style with which it was said is from here.

BORGES. Of course, and that's much more important than the words he used. It seems to me that if one insists on local colour, then everything becomes false, doesn't it? For example, I have written milongas and I've looked not for Argentinean words, although there will be some, but yes, let's say the natural cadences of the Argentinean. And I've not looked for them— they were given to me.

FERRARI. Or you looked for them in some moment.

BORGES. Yes, certainly and you will see, if you take the trouble to read my milongas, there are almost no Creole words. Some are inevitable, I haven't searched for them. I believe the Creole must be more in the cadence, in the voice. And that voice, the reader reads a text, and if the text is Creole, he reads it in a Creole style.

FERRARI. One perceives it. Now, to recapitulate, we have, for example, the well-known theory of Martínez Estrada, according to which here, it has been forcefully adapted by European culture, on a land and a people which has still not resolved questions of culture and civilization within its own country.

BORGES. Well, Vicente Rossi went much further—a *reduction ad absurdum*—he said he had chosen Spanish among other possible languages. That's untrue, of course: it is the same to maintain that one can choose between Guarani and Castilian, or between Castilian and French. Everybody is speaking Castilian. But it's that it's even rarer. For example, there's a story, 'El destino es chambón', by Arturo Cancela, in which he says that a mate, who was called López, was proud of his Spanish surname. Now, I believe that people didn't think that López was Spanish—it was a surname everybody knew. I don't think it was thought of as Spanish. They were speaking naturally, innocently.

FERRARI. Yes. On the other hand, you have said that Argentinian history can define itself as a desire to separate itself from Spain.

BORGES. Ah, yes of course, but a political separation. Now, as regards the language, well, from the moment we speak Castilian . . . the use of 'Castilian' was preferred to 'Spanish' because 'Castilian' seemed more general. And now, in Spain one says 'Spanish', because 'Castilian' appears limited to a region, Castile. But here, what can we do with Spanish regions? Nothing. Then 'Castilian' is preferred because it seems more general. In exchange, in Spain, 'Castilian' is regional. It's odd that those two words 'Castilian' and 'Spanish' should have different connotations according to if they are said this side or that side of the Atlantic. But that fact is a given, and Lugones called his dictionary a dictionary of normal usage. And there is a book by the philologist Costa Álvarez, and he talks of Castillian, Argentinian or something similar—and not of Spanish. Spanish had already seemed to him like a political interference.

FERRARI. They are nothing more than names, in any case.

BORGES. Of course

FERRARI. One of the facts that I think seemed representative to you of the natural link that there is between Argentina and Europe was the preoccupation with what followed from the alternatives of the Second World War, and the side that some and others took in that moment.

BORGES. Yes, I think we took account of our identity with Spain due to the Spanish Civil War, because, before, nobody remembered that we had been Spaniards in that epoch. But the Civil War came along and people are in favour of the Monarchy or the Republic, or better said, of Franco or the Republic.

FERRARI. And that is prolonged after the Second World War with the Alliedophiles . . .

BORGES. Yes, the Alliedophiles and the Germanophiles. I published an article and in it I said that the Germanophiles were not friends of Germany, they were simply enemies of England and France. They were not really friends of Germany of which they knew absolutely nothing.

FERRARI. Then, can you trace here at this point the misunderstanding between liberals and nationalists in the country?

BORGES. Yes, I think so, because the nationalists were, according to the Germanophiles, although they knew nothing of Germany. But, that didn't matter, what interested them was that Hitler was against England and France, above all against England. I said that in an article published in *El Hogar*.

FERRARI. But in this moment: How do you see this dilemma about whether we have our own tradition, linked, or not, to Spain or with other countries?

BORGES. No. Moreover, it's better not to talk about that.

FERRARI. Can we suppose that it has been resolved?

BORGES. The more traditions we have the better. The more we owe to different countries not excluding Spain the better. Why not accept all possible countries and cultures? Why not spread out to be cosmopolitan? There is no reason for the contrary.

FERRARI. Perhaps already now, yes, it can be said, that we have a little literary tradition in the country.

BORGES. And in the nineteenth century, since in the end, a name like Sarmiento or Almafuerte, and, why not, López and others.

FERRARI. I say this because writers of later generations, such as Murena, said the act of writing in this country is possible, starting with Borges, Mallea, Martínez Estrada and Marechal.

BORGES. Well, we are going to omit one of the names—mine. As Martínez Estrada, Lugones wrote without those privileged possibilities (*both laugh*).

FERRARI. The tradition acted, then, on others also.

BORGES. It seems so. In any case, I didn't know that. It never occurred to me to put the name Marechal next to that of Martínez Estrada.

11

Emerson and Whitman

●

OSVALDO FERRARI. There's something special, Borges, in your vision of Emerson. You say that Whitman and Poe have observed history, the history of Emerson.

JORGE LUIS BORGES. Yes, and the two were almost unknown compared with Emerson. And Emerson was very generous with Whitman. Whitman sent him the first copy . . . no, a copy of the first edition of *Leaves of Grass* in the year 1855, the year in which Longfellow published another American poem, 'Hiawatha', which has been forgotten, or relegated to the schools—which is the same. So, in the same year, the year 1855, 'Hiawatha' appeared, a kind of North American *Tabaré*, except whites don't appear, it all happens among Indians. And Longfellow took the metre of 'Kalevala', the Finnish poem but which is not a very stimulating metre. And that same year the first edition of *Leaves of Grass* appeared.

Now, Emerson had, in some way prophesized Whitman, because in an article, 'The American Scholar', he says that an American poet would have to include everything—not only the good but also the bad. The traps, the crimes, the hatred, the greed—all that, he says, would have to exist. But, of course, it's one thing to prophesy a poet and another thing to be that poet.

FERRARI. Ah, of course.

BORGES. It's completely different. Well, then Emerson sent a letter, very generous, or very justly generous, to Whitman, telling him that he believed that poem was the most ingenuous . . . with more wisdom than had been constructed up to now in our America. And he said that he rarely went to New York, but that the next time that he went, he would not lose the opportunity of extending his hand to his bene- factor, which was Whitman, for having written that book.

Whitman, I think, was editor of the *Brooklyn Eagle*, a daily, neg- ligible, but he wrote that great poem. Now Whitman acted in a way that offended Emerson—he published Emerson's letter. And that, it was understood, was bad, because it was a private letter Emerson had sent, and he had no right to do it. Moreover he had published it in the third edition where, against the opinion of Emerson, he had included erotic poems which are famous now but then . . .

FERRARI. Yes . . .

BORGES. And, naturally, Emerson, in some way, came across as an accomplice in those poems which scandalized their contemporary readers. Although now they can be published without any deteriora- tion to him, without great danger.

FERRARI. All this makes Emerson, as you see him, a true gentleman.

BORGES. Yes. I don't know if . . . I don't recall having read in the biographies of Whitman that Emerson made any reproach, but he kept apart from him. And Whitman went on publishing. Every year a new edition, with new poems. In accordance with the opinions and reflections at the beginning of the book. For Whitman, those poems, which are so different and which deal with such diverse themes—they were a single poem, a kind of epic, an American epic poem.

And the personage Whitman was really a trinity, made up of Whitman the man, Whitman magnified by the author's imagination, since we know that Whitman was born on Long Island but in the book he is sometimes born in Texas and then travels the country— but that's something that didn't happen. He shows up as miner in California, he shows up in Nebraska, but all that is Whitman's imagination. And then the third person of that trinity would be the reader who also intervenes, since Whitman converses with him and frequently addresses him. Or he makes the reader ask him things and he replies. That is to say, a very rare concept. And all that corresponded to the idea of democracy, because Whitman, in a rather rare stanza, refers to pictures in which there are personages who have godly aureoles. And he says that he wanted that, that in his poem all the personages should have aureoles, since the poem is not about a man but, well, about all Americans. And not only contemporary Americans but also future Americans, since he is also singing of them. In other words, that Walt Whitman personage is plural and virtually infinite. And it is understood that the reader is part of that poem. And that reader may be posterior to Whitman.

Good, we now in some way have been prefigured by Whitman.

FERRARI. Clearly now, your esteem for Emerson seems to me very high, because you say that in certain considered aspects, Whitman and Poe are inferior to Emerson.

BORGES. Well, of course, they are incomparable. I don't know, I think I should not have said that. They are incomparable.

FERRARI. A moment of exaltation.

BORGES. Yes, now to Emerson, Poe was decidedly disagreeable, because he called him 'the jingle man', the man of the droning, refer-ring, I suppose to the famous poem . . .

FERRARI. 'The Bells'.

BORGES. 'The Bells', and there 'The bells, bells, bells'—that seemed to Emerson an insignificant game. And he called him 'Poe, oh yes a jingle man', a man of droning. But it becomes more amusing in English because 'jingle' is already droning, isn't it?

FERRARI. 'Jingle man' is nice.

BORGES. Yes, 'Oh Poe, the jingle man' (*laughs*). Emerson was an intel-lectual poet, of course. Not a passionate poet, I should say not . . . but who knows if passion is a necessary element of poetry. It may have a type of poetry, well, if one thinks of Pope, if one thinks of Boileau, they are not poets especially passionate but they are poets. Or let's select a more illustrious example, or more antique: if one thinks about Horace, for example, one thinks rather of verbal perfection but one doesn't think of Horace as passionate. So I don't know up to what point passion is necessary. Well, emotion, yes of course, without emo-tion poetry cannot be conceived. But without passion it can be—

there is such a type, of fresh poetry, intellectual, of very lucid poetry, so, written by a very intelligent man but not a very passionate man, not necessarily passionate.

FERRARI. Except we can conjecture intellectual passion.

BORGES. Oh, in that case yes, the intellectual love of which Spinoza spoke, certainly, and Emerson didn't lack love. Now Poe: I believe he hadn't read a lot but he pretended to be very erudite. And Whitman: possibly. Well, he had read the essential books, the great epics. Whitman, of course, is inconceivable without the Bible, without the Psalms of David. But what he did was distinct, and in Whitman's verse, it is like an echo of the Psalms but more extensive, more complex. And the idea of liberty takes him to that idea of free verse. Of course, if he wanted to be the poet of democracy, he couldn't use the ancient forms. He liked to think that all before was feudal.

FERRARI. Whitman did.

BORGES. He inaugurated the poetry of democracy but that did not consist, of course, in saying 'Oh democracy', and then some flattery with rhetorical words. No, it consisted in doing something essentially different. He wrote a poem whose hero is all men, all Americans, for him. Now, Whitman insists that his book is a draft, that it is simply a point of departure for future poets, and in some way it has been so. But I don't know if it has been exceeded. I believe not.

FERRARI. Clearly, an insuperable draft.

BORGES. Yes, I believe so, I would say that of Whitman. Well, of course, Carl Sandburg could manage the colloquial language much better than Whitman. Moreover, Whitman wanted to demonstrate that he had read a lot. Whitman's preferred poet was Tennyson, a cultured poet. In exchange,, Sandburg energetically adopted the vernacular style. He could do it in a much easier way, then he was more clearly defined the American.

FERRARI. Now, always when Emerson is cited, Borges, he is associated with Carlyle—there are several links with Carlyle, or of Carlyle with Emerson. You will recall what Groussac said.

BORGES. Yes, I think that it's very unjust.

FERRARI. It's very unjust.

BORGES. What's more, Carlyle was a very unhappy man, passionate without doubt. He had a terrible vision of the world. In exchange, Emerson . . . he was a lucid man . . . and if one compares Carlyle's *Hero-Worship* with Emerson's *Representative Men*, well, they are completely different, since Carlyle only admires violent people, hard people. He admires tyrants. Carlyle wrote about Doctor Francia— an article, in short, eulogistic—and he admired Frederick of Prussia, and he would have admired Napoleon, except that Napoleon was French, and he had a love of Germany and in some way a hatred of France, although one of his best books is *The French Revolution.*

FERRARI. Always when we talk of Carlyle, you recall that phrase of his about the universal history as a sacred text.

BORGES. Yes, the universal history, that is to say, we can call it the cosmic process, yes, it says that the universal history is a text that we're always reading, always writing, and— here's the mysterious bit—in which we are written too. History is like a divine cryptography, and we ourselves are signs of that cryptography. That's what Swedenborg took, perhaps, the idea of the whole world as a cryptography. In other words, everything has a meaning. And, of course, that has to be derived from the idea of the Bible, doesn't it? Of the idea that the Bible, well . . . Dante thinks about four possible readings of the Bible. In the Middle Ages this was thought and, what's more, in four possible readings of his *Divine Comedy*.

FERRARI. Yes. Now to prove your admiration for Emerson, I'd like to read your poem to Emerson, if you agree.

BORGES. The only thing I know is that it's unworthy of Emerson, and that Ezequiel Martínez Estrada wrote a very superior poem. But let's look at mine.

FERRARI. Let's look at yours: 'Closing the heavy volume of Montaigne, / The tall New Englander goes out / Into an evening which exalts the fields. / It is a pleasure worth no less than reading. / He walks towards the final sloping of the sun, / Towards the landscape's gilded edge; / He moves through darkening fields as he moves now / Through the memory of the one who writes this down' . . .

BORGES. And, this one, that's not bad.

FERRARI. Nothing wrong with that.

BORGES. Although written by me.

FERRARI. It deals in this last verse with your own memory.

BORGES. Yes.

FERRARI. 'He thinks: I have read the essential books / And written others which oblivion / Will not efface. I have been allowed / That which is given mortal man to know. / The whole continent knows my name. / I have not lived. I want to be someone else.'

BORGES. There's a poem of his, 'Days', in which he says the same, in which the days pass and that he rejects them, because he refused the delights of life. He has simply limited himself and intellectual delight, as you said. He was repentant about that in the end.

FERRARI. However . . .

BORGES. There remains in him a kind of calm happiness.

FERRARI. Yes, I think so. Moreover he was a very intelligent man, a man who was always thinking how he was not going to be happy. Stupid people are unhappy. A man who is reflecting, who is, well, renovating the past each time he recalls it, who is changing his opinion, that intellectual activity has to be a form of happiness. And Emerson certainly had it.

12

Stoicism

•

OSVALDO FERRARI. I always thought your habits of life, Borges, which are austere, are related, not to mystical asceticism but to philosophical stoicism.

JORGE LUIS BORGES. Yes, of course. In contrast to Manuel Mujica Lainez, for example, luxury seems to me horrible. I don't know . . . there's something . . . well, maybe my Methodist upbringing. The thing is, I feel luxury as a kind of stupid remark, don't you know. It seems to me vulgar.

FERRARI. Almost like a waste of time.

BORGES. And many people don't, don't feel that, but I do. The same thing happens to me with language—it seems to me convenient to avoid luxurious language and luxurious descriptions.

FERRARI. Certainly, one can say, if there's something you can't be, it's baroque.

BORGES. Well, no. I was once, for a long time, but now no longer. So that I could repeat those verses, perhaps the best in the Castilian tongue, the letter of the anonymous Sevillian which they now attribute to a Captain Fernández de Andrada, but it would be better if the poem continues being anonymous, because it's what he would have wished. And the verses are—Alfonso Reyes quotes them and says something about 'supreme elegance'—let's suppress the 'supreme', which is also a small change, don't you think (*laughs*): 'An average life I possess / a moderate and common style / which nobody who sees it notes'.

I don't know if I have the right to consider myself, well, let's say, stoical or relatively simple. I think not, because on what really interests me, which are books, I spend a lot. And that's a little absurd since I can't read them. Which is to say, it's an illusory acquisition. Now Schopenhauer said that one should acquire with the book the necessary time to read it. But what happens is that the possession of a book is confused with possession of the book's content, and throughout one is not very sure—above all in the case of novels—one isn't very sure about having read it, or not. For example, now, evening after evening, I'm used to going to the academy . . . and then talking about the Errázuriz Palace. The word 'palace' seems to me very, very vulgar. Not in Italy, perhaps, since there are many palaces, and the palaces tend to be rather ascetic and beautiful. But not here, here a palace gives the idea of ostentation. Now, in the case of Mujica Lainez, I think he takes into account that this was a bit vulgar. At the same time, it amused him. Similarly, he had to know that the fact of multiplying ties and rings is a bit flashy, no? At the same time, it amused him.

I like walking sticks, but I think I have no more than five or six. Whereas I believe Mujica Lainez has sixty or seventy. One who also had lots of sticks—those sticks varied according to the time of day and clothing—was Henry James. Wells, for example, recounts that for the morning there was a certain stick for a certain suit which could serve for 'a morning call'. On the other hand, I don't know . . . the splendour of sundown chooses a splendour of clothing also. When I was a professor in the Argentinean Association of English Culture, I thought, I felt: Better said, that a writer didn't have to bother about his clothes. What I didn't know was that the students greatly pitied me, because they saw me as a man with one jacket, one pair of pants, one pair of shoes, one tie and two shirts. They had made that computation, and I didn't know I had been reduced to that (*laughs*). But the truth is that, generally, only when something is worn out do I buy something new. Maybe at that time people were simpler . . .

I don't know if I told you that it was once discussed, it was affirmed and denied, the fact of Carlos Alberto Erro y Eduardo Mallea standing in front of a shop window, looking at and comparing overcoats. And that seemed very strange, above all in the case of writers. Not now, though, for I believe everybody talks about clothes . . . and why not? Oscar Wilde said that a reform in style is more important than a reform in ethics, didn't he? But in the end, it's one of Wilde's 'reforms'.

FERRARI. He also said that the first serious step in life is to know how properly to knot your tie. And you—I think you were referring to Lugones—said that when he squared up as a poet, he was always a bit of a dandy.

BORGES. In the case of Lugones?

FERRARI. I think you referred to that when conjecturing about the moments before the suicide.

BORGES. No, I referred to Francisco López Merino.

FERRARI. Oh, López Merino.

BORGES. No, not to Lugones. He killed himself in front of a mirror.

FERRARI. Lugones or López Merino?

BORGES. López Merino, in the basement of the La Plata Jockey Club. But not Lugones. About Lugones, I've the impression that he dressed himself decorously, didn't he? although not with decorous humility. But why not give importance to everything? And we have as an exemplary case of a poet who was a dandy in Petronius, called Arbiter Elegantiarum, arbiter of elegance, and that reminds us of Wilde. He says that he could give an opinion about everything, from such a thing as a toga or about the correct handling of a stick.

FERRARI. Inside Wilde's century and close to Wilde, we can see Poe or Baudelaire, for whom dandyism was very important.

BORGES. I didn't know that about Poe.

FERRARI. Baudelaire speaks of Poe as a dandy, not only in his dress but also in his character.

BORGES. And there's a phrase of Baudelaire, which seems a little uncanny, you can say there's a kind of horror in the phrase. But I don't know if he thought that, he thought rather that everything in life had to be conscious. Baudelaire said: 'To live and to die before a mirror.' To live and die in front of a mirror, which is somewhat terrible, isn't it? The idea of that, well, it continues, the crystalline and silent vigilance of the mirror.

FERRARI. Certainly, but I found, Borges, all along, some other coincidences of yours with stoicism. For example, in your idea of living this life in a determined way and not to be too much preoccupied with the other life.

BORGES. Well, that was said by Confucius and he certainly wasn't a Stoic. He said—and I believe he said it without malice—it's necessary to respect supernatural beings, but better to keep them at a distance (*both laugh*). Now, that doesn't mean that he disbelieved them. He thought that . . . or as the Shinto says, 'One life at a time', that is to say, let us conduct ourselves correctly in this life and not worry about our conduct in the other. Some days ago, I was told something very strange about I don't know what tribe of redskins in the United States. It wasn't one of the famous tribes, it wasn't, for example, the Comanche, the Sioux or the Mohicans . . . it seems every morning, the family recounted its dreams, and fathers taught their sons how they must conduct themselves in their dreams.

This can be capable of two interpretations: one, which is the least interesting, is to suppose that if one bears himself well in a dream, he will bear himself well when awake. The other would be more lovely: to suppose that dreams are not less real than wakefulness or that wakefulness is a form of dream. Now, it seems that in certain primitive societies, it is supposed that when a man dreams, he travels, and, therefore, in the dream, he is in distant places and he meets beings whom he will not see again because he has travelled very far.

FERRARI. That idea is very lovely.

BORGES. It's a lovely idea, yes, but we should have these two interpretations. One, that if one is upright, he must be upright in dreams. But the other would be nicer—the other would be, well, that there's no frontier between wakefulness and dreams.

FERRARI. That life is a dream, no less.

BORGES. Life is a dream. Kant said (he was an idealist), that the difference—and this has been noted and censured by Schopenhauer—is that the acts we commit in dreams don't have karma, that is to say, they don't produce any effect. On the other hand, in life they do. It means that if you kill someone in a dream, the following morning that person isn't dead. Or if someone enters your house the following morning you discover that nobody has entered.

FERRARI. Of course.

BORGES. But that would not be a true difference since, in the long run, we don't know if our acts have any consequence. That is to say, if we think about infinite time, what we ourselves live is no less momentary than what we dream—our wakefulness is no less momentary than our dream. So that I don't know what difference we could establish.

FERRARI. One has to see. Now, as regards to the preoccupation for the ethical, Borges, it's constant among all the stoics. Above all, with Marcus Aurelius. There is almost a sublime preoccupation with the ethical in him.

BORGES. There's a very nice phrase of Marcus Aurelius, that is in *Meditations*, which lends itself to an interpretation . . . well, a humourous interpretation, completely alien to Marcus Aurelius' thought: 'One can live well, even in a palace.' Now, that does not mean that one can live comfortably even in a palace—it means one can live correctly even in a palace. Perhaps it may be more difficult to live correctly in a palace than, well, in a little convent, because the palace offers more temptations, isn't that so?

FERRARI. That's splendid coming from him, eh?

BORGES. Yes, of course, because he lived in palaces.

FERRARI. He was nothing less than an emperor.

BORGES. Nothing less than emperor, the palace was his quotidian habitat.

FERRARI. Note that Simone Weil, for example, who always stresses the superiority of the Greek culture over the Roman, makes, however, one exception, with Marcus Aurelius.

BORGES. Well, of course, in Roman culture there was a certain vulgarity: the gigantism of the Coliseum, for example. And then the lies of the emperors, which are unbelievable, no? Now, the decadence of Greece would have begun with Alexander of Macedonia. He was contaminated with Asiatic ideas, with Oriental ideas. The very idea of an empire seemed all right to the Greeks.

FERRARI. Yes, now, in the *Meditations* of Marcus Aurelius, to whom we referred, the formation of a resistant soul is dealt with, let's say, to the disgraces, to the temptations, and suitable for complying with the duties. In other words, with the stoical idea of life.

BORGES. One who was a stoic poet, in some way, would be, in this country, Almafuerte. He's the only poet who was interested in the ethical.

FERRARI. Yes.

BORGES. And in thought, also. In the case of Lugones, for example, what, above all interested him was form. That is to say, he has a baroque style but not a baroque sentiment. Lugones, it seems to me, is a man of elemental ideas. So there's a disparity between the complexity of the style and that essential simplicity.

FERRARI. It's that the Argentinian spirit would have some affinity with the stoical spirit, in the best of cases.

BORGES. And if only it were so, of course. I have observed, throughout my overlong life, regarding intelligence, goodness, justice, one feels it immediately. Not through but in spite of words and acts. One can feel that a person is intelligent though that person can have spoken trivialities. A person can have said intelligent things, yet one can think that essentially he is stupid.

FERRARI. How important this is, what you are saying.

BORGES. Furthermore, I will have told you more than once: the transmission of thought isn't a rare event, it is something that occurs continually. When one reads a book also, one can be not in agreement with everything—one can be uninterested in the story, one can think the book's action is clumsily managed, but one can feel sympathy for the author, or antipathy.

FERRARI. Something that is beyond words has been caught.

BORGES. I think so. Yesterday I was writing a prologue to the essay by Atilio Momigliano on *Orlando Furioso* and he says that Ariosto arouses sympathy but not veneration. And doubtless when he wrote those words he was thinking of Dante. Because Dante arouses veneration but not sympathy. A proof would be: if by some miracle a dialogue with Dante was proposed to us, we'd be somewhat terrified. In contrast, it would be very lovely to converse with Ariosto or to converse, why not, let's be ambitious, to converse with Wilde.

FERRARI. It would be magnificent, absolutely.

BORGES. But a dialogue with Dante, how would it be? Either it would be an elegant plaintive moan on his part, or a bit like a conversation . . . like a catechism.

FERRARI. More admirable than amiable, should we say.

BORGES. Yes, I think so.

FERRARI. In the pessimism and scepticism characteristic of the stoical doctrine, I do find, Borges, a great affinity with you. For example, if I ask you whether God is or is not just, I have my doubts about your reply.

BORGES. With me you have been at times very generous, but I think at times unjust. I don't know if I deserve, after having loved books so much, to be an illiterate since 1955. I think not.

FERRARI. One sees that very well in your 'Poem of the Gifts'.

BORGES. Everybody tells me that I do not, precisely, see, because I see inwardly, but these are games with words. That is using the word 'see' with two different meanings because, in fact, a blind man does not see. And the fact that he intuits, or that he takes account of certain things, does not replace the continuous pleasure of the physical world.

FERRARI. Moreover, in one of your latest poems 'On His Blindness' you say: 'I should like / Once to see a face.'

BORGES. Yes, but possibly, saying that, I wasn't being sincere.

13

Jesus Christ

●

OSVALDO FERRARI. We have, Borges, referred before, although always occasionally, to Catholicism and Protestantism, but we have never talked about your way of seeing the figure that is the origin of them, the figure of Christ.

JORGE LUIS BORGES. I said—Renan has already said it much better than I—that if Christ is not the human incarnation of God—which seems extremely unlikely—then he was in some way the most extraordinary man that history has recorded. Now, I don't know if it has ever been observed that Christ is, among so many other things, a literary style. You read Milton's *Paradise Lost* and *Paradise Regained* and, as Pope said, they are the Father and the Son debating like scholastics. Christ's style is an extraordinary style. We think that, for centuries, writers have searched for metaphors. More recently, Lugones and Góngara . . . we could mention many others. But nobody has found images as extraordinary as those of Christ, images that even after two thousand years continue to be astonishing. For example: 'To cast pearls before swine'—how could he arrive at that phrase? For the majority of the phrases, one thinks: Good, he has reached them through variations, but to cast pearls before swine is a phrase that goes on being extraordinary, and which one can't classify, and which is illogical. Or, if not, for example, to condemn funeral rites, which the funeral parlours are so fond of, seconded by the churches. That 'Let the dead bury their dead.' That makes it terrible and, moreover, suggests a fantastic explanation. Or 'That he who is not guilty, let him throw the first stone'.

FERRARI. It's always valid.

BORGES. Now, that should justify what the English mystic William Blake said—he had always thought that salvation was an ethical process, and that it was encouraged, demagogically, let's say, by Christ himself when he said, 'Blessed are the poor in spirit because of them will be the Kingdom of Heaven.' In other words, he insisted on behaviour.

But then along comes the Swedish mystic Swedenborg. Swedenborg says that salvation has also to be intellectual, and he invents that splendid parable of a man who wants to enter Heaven. Then he renounces everything, he lives in solitude. Or in his solitude, he renounces all sensual, intellectual and aesthetic pleasures. He lives virtuously, he martyrs himself and effectively reaches Heaven, since there is not any reason to refuse him. But when he arrives, he finds himself in a world much more complex than this one, since, according to Swedenborg, there are in Heaven more shapes, more colours and of course more intelligence than here. And the poor man, who is only a saint, has to attend the dialogues of the angels. According to Swedenborg's *Of Heaven and Hell*, the angels discuss theology. So he understands nothing, since he has not educated his intelligence. So he feels that in some way he is excluded from Heaven. Then the authorities, let's say, become aware of that, and say: 'What can we do with him? In Heaven he is lost since he cannot participate in angelic dialogues. But to send him to Hell among the devils would be obviously unjust.' Then they reach this melancholy solution: they let him project in the other world an image of his solitude. And there that man is, in this moment alone, he sees that illusory desert which he needs, he continues mortifying himself and praying. But mortifying himself and praying now without hope, because he knows that he can no longer aspire to Heaven.

FERRARI. Oh, but how curious.

BORGES. A terrible fate. Well, along comes Blake, and Blake says the salvation of man has to be not only ethical, as it emerges from Christ's teaching, and not only intellectual, as it comes from Swedenborg's teaching. But he says directly: 'The fool shall not enter Heaven be he ever so holy.' And in another sentence in *Marriage of Heaven and Hell*, he says: 'Put off holiness and put on intellect.' (*Both laugh*) Now, according to Blake, there's also an aesthetic teaching by Christ. That teaching was, before everything else, a literary teaching, and that is given by the parables of Christ, which are literary pieces, pieces that have not been imitated. I thought some days ago—I'm going to confide in you this project of mine, maybe you can carry it out, I certainly can't. It was to become the maximum ambition for a writer— writers are usually very ambitious—something much more ambitious than to write . . . the deliberately obscure work of Góngara or that rather unjustifiable labyrinth *Finnegan's Wake* by Joyce . . . well, the project was to be this: it would be to write a fifth Gospel. That fifth Gospel would predicate an ethic which was not that of the other Gospels. But the most difficult would not be that. The most difficult would be to invent new parables, said in the manner of Christ and saying things which were not in the other four Gospels.

FERRARI. To prolong in some way . . .

BORGES. If a writer manages to do that, it would be much more extraordinary than Nietzsche's *Thus Spake Zarathustra*, since it would come to be . . . well, having to create works of art, you would have to create risky metaphors, no less extraordinary than what was preached in Galilee. To end up with a book, a writer would have to dedicate a good part of his life to meditation, and then to the editing of his books. And that Gospel would have to have some thirty pages and would be one of the most extraordinary books. And if that book were lucky, it would be printed along with the Gospels of the New Testament. But it's a very ambitious project, and you, Ferrari, can perhaps . . . I, of course, am an old man, and very tired—but I begin to see that beautiful literary possibility, more beautiful than the possibility of making books with new metaphors, because those metaphors would have to be parables, teachings that compare favourably with those of the already immortal and famous New Testament.

FERRARI. Your proposal coincides with a proposal of Kierkegaard who says that to be a Christian is equivalent to becoming Christ's contemporary.

BORGES. Good, and that coincides with the book by Kempis, *Imitation of Christ*.

FERRARI. Ah, of course.

BORGES. Clearly, it would come to be similar but it would a lovely task, and it's possible, while I speak, there's someone out there who is performing it.

FERRARI. Probably.

BORGES. Because it would be very difficult that something new would occur to somebody. That will never happen. This, which has occurred to me will already have occurred to someone else, above all others I have read. But in that case, no, a new, a fifth Gospel would be a lovely task and it would not disgrace the four earlier ones. It would sometimes coincide with them, at others disagree, for greater pleasure, for greater surprise, for greater verisimilitude of text. Now, for example, how strange that the Christian faith condemns suicide. However, if the Gospels have meaning, the death of Christ was voluntary. Because if it was not voluntary, what sacrifice is that?

FERRARI. We could think the same about the death of Socrates.

BORGES. Yes, but in the case of Socrates, I don't believe he said that he died for humanity, but in the case of Christ, yes. And if he died, he died freely. Now, there's an Anglo-Saxon poem of the ninth century, 'The Dream of the Cross'. And in the dream of the cross, Christ appears not as the suffering Christ of the canvases of El Greco but as a young Germanic hero who voluntarily reaches the cross, he climbs the cross because he wants to save men, and when they speak of him, they say: 'This young hero, who was God Almighty.' That is to say, there's the idea of a happy and voluntary sacrifice—not of a passion suffered by a Christ, the suffering like in the canvases of El Greco. No, this is the young hero who was nailed to the cross or who climbed it. And I have read in some note about that poem that there are medieval illustrations in which one sees the cross, already erected, already standing, and Christ climbing a ladder, indicating that he does it deliberately. In other words, all the contrary to, well, to Golgotha, the scourging . . .

FERRARI. Therefore it's said that there's something similar in the acceptance of the cross by Christ and the hemlock by Socrates.

BORGES. It's certain, yes.

FERRARI. In the attitude of acceptance.

BORGES. And, of course, they are the two deaths most recorded in history, aren't they?

FERRARI. Probably. Now . . .

BORGES. The conversational death of Socrates, and the death of Christ who is somewhat astonished by his fate, since his human side says: 'Lord, Lord, why hast thou forsaken me?' But later he says to the thief: 'This night you will be with me in Paradise.' And the thief accepts that. I have written a poem, well, many have written poems about Christ and about the thief who from the neighbouring cross accepts that Christ is God.

FERRARI. About Barrabas and Christ.

BORGES. Yes.

FERRARI. Now, it always seemed to me, Borges, that for you the archetype, the model man, would be the archetype of the just man.

BORGES. I try to be just but, of course, I don't expect, well, like Spinoza, any recompense, and I don't fear any punishment.

FERRARI. Of course, but the archetype of the just man is, precisely, the ethical archetype.

BORGES. Yes, of course. I have been brought up hearing the Gospels. I believe they are the most extraordinary books in the world, the four Gospels. And the last already has a different character, a character so intellectual, no?, when it speaks of the Word, for example.

FERRARI. Now, the ethic of Christ, and the ethic of Socrates . . . In Christ one is dealing with a religious ethic, and in Socrates with a profane ethic. However, I'd say they coincide in the fundamental— in the ideal of the just man.

BORGES. Yes, but in the concept of the world, no. And it's natural that it be so, because I suppose that Christ would be a Jew . . . and, perhaps, rather ignorant. While Socrates lived in that intense intellectual environment of Greece, perhaps never equalled. Socrates, it seems, could converse with Pythagoras, with Zenon of Elea and with Plato who, according to Shaw, invented him. In exchange, Christ, was with his disciples. Now, Nietzsche said that the Christian religion was a religion of slaves. And Gibbon said, indirectly and perhaps more effectively, the same: 'It must amaze us that God, who could have revealed the truth to philosophers, revealed it to some ignorant fishermen in Galilee.' It comes to be the same idea, but said in a way, well, more polite and more insidious.

FERRARI. 'The spirit blows where it will.'

BORGES. Yes, it's the spirit that blows where it wants, yes. In that case it blew for, well, those poor men.

FERRARI. Now, it seems unreal for a moment, although with you less so, to speak about the figure of Christ as a historical figure.

BORGES. I think there's no doubt about that, because if not we have to suppose, let's say, four dramaturges, very superior to all other dramaturges and to all the other poets of the world, believing in that figure. Now Shaw believed. Shaw spoke of the apostolic succession, and he spoke of, well, the Greek tragedians who had created the Greek myths. Then the evangelists had created the figure of Christ, and already, earlier, Plato had created the figure of Socrates. And then Boswell had created Johnson, and Shaw and Ibsen had inherited the apostolic succession of drama as the creator of personages. But it's another of Shaw's jokes.

FERRARI. The world as theatre.

BORGES. The world as theatre, and the dramaturges as . . .

FERRARI. As demi-urges.

BORGES. As demi-urges and as providers of universal history.

FERRARI. The other figure who at times it is hard to see historically, as it's hard with Christ, is Plato. I think we imagine Plato more than we represent him.

BORGES. Plato is ramified in so many personages, and among them Socrates, it seems that he himself has been a bit erased by his creatures. A lesser case . . . well, I don't know if one imagines Dickens or if one imagines the characters of Dickens. I think that Unamuno has said that Cervantes is less lived than Alonso Quijano, than Don Quixote. That is to say, the creator has been erased by his work. And in the case of the world, perhaps we have a more vivid impression of the world than of the God in the first chapter of Genesis, no?

FERRARI. Of course, but we could also think that men believe in a religion, or in a mythology, according to the spiritual or magical climate in which they are immersed. For example, the Greeks were able to accept Plato's ideas in his time because in Greek life poetry was a form of the reality they were living.

BORGES. Does it seem to you that it is more difficult now?

FERRARI. And in the same way, the conjecture. Well, the conjecture isn't mine, it's Murena's. He said that Christ's contemporaries were able to have seen and recognized because they had their eyes open to a similar reality. That is, it depends on that historic moment, among men, on a certain climate for perceiving things.

BORGES. You are saying a climate of credulity, or of perception.

FERRARI. Probably a spiritual climate.

BORGES. Yes, I have the impression that almost everybody now lives, well, as if they don't see, that there is like a . . . I don't know, they have bloated their senses, isn't that so? I have that impression.

FERRARI. Spiritual meanings have become bloated, in any case.

BORGES. Yes, things are not felt. People live by hearsay . . . above all, they repeat formulas but don't try to imagine them, nor do they draw any conclusions about them. It seems that they live thus, receiving, but receiving in a superficial way. It is as if nobody will think, as if reason is a habit men are losing.

FERRARI. Above all, the spiritual intelligence of things. At the most, logic is used, but nothing more. And in the better of cases.

BORGES. Yes, in the better of cases, since that seems difficult also, that people reason.

FERRARI. Catholic or Protestant, believers and non-believers. I think, Borges, that the figure of Christ is always constructive and useful.

BORGES. Yes, and he hasn't been substituted, because Nietzsche's project of replacing him by Zarathustra has failed, well, famously, but it has failed, of course.

FERRARI. The project of the Antichrist.

BORGES. Yes, all of them. Well, Zarathustra was one of the most ambitious. Of course, that has failed, since nobody thinks about Zarathustra, in his lion who laughs, in his eagle, in his crow. All that is evidently a joke, I shouldn't say joke but a somewhat clumsy literary affection, isn't that so?

FERRARI. Yes, that's so, he who said 'God is dead' has not managed to replace him.

BORGES. No, it appears not, that voice one heard, saying that Pan had died. It seems that he has not been replaced.

14

Apology for Friendship

●

OSVALDO FERRARI. No one has made, as far as I know, Borges, an apology for friendship in the country, like what you have made over time.

JORGE LUIS BORGES. I hadn't, however, known that it was possible. I told you that when I read Mallea's book *History of an Argentinian Passion*, I thought: That passion has to be friendship, since there's no other passion here. Then it happened that it wasn't. And then, without doubt, we've spoken of the theme of friendship throughout our brief literature. I don't know if you have observed that the true theme of Estanislao del Campo's *Faust* is not the parody of the opera—the true theme is the friendship of the two sharecroppers. Isn't it?

FERRARI. Yes, in *Faust*, you tell us that there is 'a happy sentiment of friendship'.

BORGES. Oh, I think so. And the theme of *Don Segundo Sombra* is the same. And perhaps the essential theme of *Martín Fierro* would also be that strange friendship between a policeman and a deserter, isn't that so?—of Cruz and Fierro?

FERRARI. I was sure you were going to see that.

BORGES. Yes, and then there's a book which I haven't read by Eduardo Gutiérrez: *A Friendship Until Death*. Well, that title sounds more or less natural alongside books such as *Black Ant* or *The Barrientos Brothers* which are related with the theme of friendship.

FERRARI. Within literature, we also find the friendship of Don Segundo and Fabio.

BORGES. It's certain. He's called Fabio? Of course, Fabio Cáceres.

FERRARI. Exactly.

BORGES. It's strange those things that one doesn't know one knows, isn't it?

FERRARI. One doesn't know what one knows. But you attribute illustrious antecedents to that friendship.

BORGES. Yes, I believe I was thinking of *Huckleberry Finn* and *Kim*.

FERRARI. In Twain and in Kipling.

BORGES. Yes. Now I don't know if Güiraldes read Twain, possibly not, but without doubt he read Kipling, because when they presented me to him, he said: They have told me that you know English. To know English in those years was something, well, much rarer than now. I said yes and he said: How lucky, you can read Kipling in the original. Yes, he spoke to me about Kipling. He would have read him in some French version, doubtless.

FERRARI. I suspect that Güiraldes, in his personal life, also made a kind of cult of friendship.

BORGES. Oh yes, of course. Without doubt. Once they came to lunch at home—Ricardo Güiraldes and Adelina del Carril—and then, a long lunch and conversation later, they left. My mother called after them because he had left the guitar—he didn't take the guitar. But he told her he'd left it on purpose—since he was going to Europe, he wanted something of his to remain in the house. And he left the guitar. And many people who came to the house played Ricardo Güiraldes' guitar.

FERRARI. A very lovely gesture on his part.

BORGES. A very fine gesture, yes. And I remember when he was writing *Don Segundo Sombra*, we went to see him in his house, near the Plaze del Congreso. It was a rather strange flat because the furniture was fitted in the walls. So when one touched a button, a chair fell out or a bed. It was in Solís Street . . . I think it was Solís and Alsina, but I'm not completely sure. I don't know if the house still exists. They took that house just before a journey to Europe. It was a fairly simple house and I think it was the only time he lived in the south. Well, south, speaking modestly, let's say, because it was two blocks from the Plaza del Congreso. He was then writing the major Estancia book, his novel *Don Segundo Sombra*. But as he was very idle, he immediately left the text and talked to us or played the guitar. And then Adelina asked us to go, because any pretext was good for him to stop writing, no?

FERRARI. His wife helped him to concentrate and to write the book.

BORGES. Yes, exactly. Clearly, if I were Néstor Ibarra, I'd say she had a fine literary sense and she wanted to prevent his writing *Don Segundo Sombra*, didn't she? (*Laughs*) But that doesn't occur to me, it occurs to Ibarra, as I imagine her, not to me. It would have been a pity if he hadn't written the book.

FERRARI. Truly. Regarding the value of friendship among the Argentinians, you say it's one or perhaps our only virtue.

BORGES. Yes, but it's a dangerous virtue, because that can easily carry us to 'Caudillismo' which comes to be like a form of friendship, doesn't it?

FERRARI. Obligated?

BORGES. Yes, if people are loyal not to the ethical, or to certain opinions, but to a man or a friend. So that, let's say, that beautiful passion lends itself to abuses.

FERRARI. I understand.

BORGES. As happens with everything, and that in some way would explain one of the bad habits of South American history: dictatorships, which easily can be helped by friends, and by friends not always interested.

FERRARI. In that case we're dealing not with friendship but with 'cronyism'.

BORGES. Yes.

FERRARI. Prejudicial 'cronyism'.

BORGES. Yes, it can bc cronyism, as you say, yes, it's a good neologism, since it establishes a difference between the two things.

FERRARI. Now, do you think, Borges, that perhaps our geographic and historical isolation. could have contributed to the development of the sentiment of friendship among us?

BORGES. Maybe also the fact that a good number of Argentineans, above all when the country was cattle-raising, were accustomed to living in solitude, or simply with the company of neighbours. Because what would have been life on a ranch . . . well, the landowners were not very different from the ranch hands, were they? The bosses weren't very different from the gauchos.

FERRARI. Solitude defined them.

BORGES. Yes, I think so, and now it seems we have lost that capacity for solitude, which without doubt we had before, and which the English have, since the English very much like solitude. I believe Lawrence says that the English have 'a hunger for lonely places'. I proved that when I was in Scotland. They said to me: 'We lead you to the loneliest place in Scotland.' And it was a very lonely place. I thought: How strange, I come from South America, they speak to me of lonely places as meritorious and admirable. Something that doesn't happen here, because people don't resign themselves to solitude now. Everyone . . . even those who live in Córdoba or in Rosario, wants to live in Buenos Aires. And in Buenos Aires, we want to live in Europe, so it seems we are always condemned not to be . . . (*laughs*).

FERRARI (*laughs*). . . . Not to be where we are.

BORGES. Where we are or where we want to be, yes.

FERRARI. A strange aspect is, I think, that we are capable of individual friendships . . .

BORGES. Oh, I think so.

FERRARI. But not that friendship of group that we call community, isn't that right?

BORGES. Which is the most important. For a country, it's the most important.

FERRARI. Naturally.

BORGES. Because the other, well, before there were rivalries between the districts, now that has steered towards football, curiously, no?

FERRARI. In any case, anything is a good pretext for division between us.

BORGES. That is certain. The truth is we have abused that pretext, that motive. Yes, there isn't a sense of community.

FERRARI. There isn't, and perhaps the country hasn't progressed as it should, precisely because of that aspect.

BORGES. Of course, that is a kind of lack of the ethical, because one thinks in terms of so-and-so, and that somebody tends to be oneself . . . and in function of the ethical which is too abstract and general.

FERRARI. Clearly, in function of oneself, of one's group or metier, but not of the country as a whole. Could we say that the type of friendship we cultivate belongs to the type of individualism you have seen in the Argentinean?

BORGES. Well, our individualism could have been a good characteristic, but I don't know if we have known how to take advantage of that characteristic. I think not. Although politics can't take advantage of it, since it consists of precisely the contrary.

15

Paul Valéry

●

OSVALDO FERRARI. In one of your pages, Borges, that you often say seem to be written by another, one reads: 'Paul Valéry is a symbol of Europe and its delicate twilight; Whitman of morning in America.' You seem to see in these two poets an extreme antagonism.

JORGE LUIS BORGES. Yes, I'd forgotten that phrase, although now I'd choose some poet who pleases me more than Valéry. Above all, to put him joined to Whitman is almost blasphemy, isn't it? Since, well, Whitman is incomparable, and Valéry I believe isn't. Now, it's clear that in a 'delicate twilight' there was maybe the idea of a decline of Europe.

FERRARI. Evidently.

BORGES. And that decline . . . I don't know if Europe has declined, but it seems what has declined is, unfortunately, the interest of the world in Europe. That doesn't mean that Europe has declined essentially but, yes, we think of Europe less. Before, nostalgia for Europe— especially for France—was something continuous. Now people can think of other lands, of other epochs . . . I suppose that what I wanted to say was that.

I would not now choose Valéry. Well, of course, there are splendid verses in Valéry. I would record before all this: 'As fruit is dissolved in taste / in a mouth in which form dies.' It's lovely because it passes from one sense to another, doesn't it? When one says 'fruit', one doesn't think of the taste but, above all, of the form and the colour. But there one passes very cleverly, admirably, from one sense to another: 'fruit dissolves in taste'. That taste which corresponds to our palate, to our tongue—and not to the fruit. And then 'in a mouth in which form dies'.

I have chosen, doubtless, one of Valéry's better verses, but that same poem begins with an image which is completely false, in that it compares the sea with a ceiling on which doves walk. And I think that if there's something which the sea does not resemble, it is that— particularly if we think of doves as a trite metaphor for sails.

Now, it's very difficult to express the sea. Perhaps the best way to do so would be not through metaphors but through a cadence similar the movement of the sea. And here I inevitably recall that verse of Kipling: 'Who has not desired the sea / the sight of salt water unbounded.' Here, the words don't matter—what matters is the rhythm.

Moreover, Valéry's description—a description I'm not sure can be logically justified but aesthetically perhaps can be—of the sea, even the small Mediterranean with its calm roof, is a false image.

FERRARI. A little arbitrary.

BORGES. In any case, it's not of major emotional efficacy. But I think I don't have to repent too much for these two lines of mine. Moreover, we have 'delicate twilight': clearly, they are two words almost synonymous, since the word twilight is delicate—above all, in Castilian in which it is a proparoxytone—which is a form of delicacy also. And then, 'the morning in America' already awakens a vast image. And, how strange, that I had completely forgotten that, and written afterwards a poem in which I thank God for many things, and I thank him 'For the morning in Texas'—this refers to the year 1961, when my mother and I discover America . . . we began with Austin, Texas. And later, the morning in Montevideo also, which always delights me—it could be mornings of the peninsula, from the Paso del Molino, from where I went—but, finally, I repeated that, and I chose two places that I love: Montevideo—the Oriental Republic—and Texas. I don't know if you know that I am an honorary citizen of Austin and of Androgue. I don't know what these things signify but, of course, they are symbols of friendship, of goodwill. And since maybe we are symbols, why not be thankful for benevolent symbols, symbols of friendship. But, you wanted us to speak especially about that line, or . . .

FERRARI. No, I had the impression that you saw in Valéry the world of the mind, the Apollonian world, in comparison with the almost Dionysian world of Whitman.

BORGES. It's a lovely idea, but I don't know how much Valéry deserves that fame he has of being an intellectual poet, since there very few ideas in his poems. I'd say, for me the archetype of an intellectual poet would be, of course, a greater name than that of Valéry: Emerson, who not only was intellectual but who, moreover, thought, which seems rare in an intellectual poet. In the case of Valéry, it seems he's called an intellectual poet, but major ideas in his poems are not noted. In any case, I don't think Valéry took thought as a poetic theme or thought while he poeticized. He thought about metre, about images and about rhyme. But that is something else, since all poets do.

FERRARI. I'm going to quote it to you: you thought in that moment, according to your words, that Valéry preferred the lucid pleasures of thought and the secret adventures of order. And I think that those are the adventures of literature, the adventures of writing in some way.

BORGES. That's certain, but I think that in that article of mine entitled 'Valéry as Symbol', I thought less about what Valéry was than, let's say, about the way in which Valéry has been accepted. That is to say, he's seen as an intellectual poet. Now the fact that he—as Adolfo Bioy Casares said—suggested thought to others but abstained from thought himself . . . (*laughs*). Maybe Bioy Casares exaggerates a bit, but it's perhaps convenient to exaggerate in any affirmation, or in any negation, so that it can be more effective. Since the reader will later take care to deduce, to polish the excesses of veneration, or the excesses of, well, I shouldn't say contempt, that's very strong, let's say, of censure, of disagreement, of difference. I remind myself of those admirable titles of Alfonso Reyes: one of his books is entitled *Sympathies and Differences*. But before that book was published, a book came out in Spain whose title is a parody, an involuntary and prophetic parody of the Reyes title. Instead of *Sympathies and Differences,* an author whom I haven't read, Bonafú, wrote a book titled *Butts and Sticks (both laugh)* which comes to be a very coarse version of saying *Sympathies and Differences.* And that coarseness was, without doubt, voluntary and fond, wasn't it? Since nobody even absentmindedly comes up with a title as ugly as *Butts and Sticks.* Moreover, it seems that butts lose all their efficacy if they are called butts, and sticks too. In other words, they correspond to the desire to approve something, and to condemn something else.

FERRARI. I see. Now what interests me is the fact that you stress other writers, Valéry's contemporaries, did not have behind them, as he does, a personality.

BORGES. That's true, yes.

FERRARI. But maybe you saw that personality projected by Valéry's work.

BORGES. And, moreover, by the fact that he left us that work, when what was being pondered was, rather, irrationality, chaos—we remember that adventure, somewhat humorous, of Dadaism—and, later, of Surrealism. All that becomes the contrary. In exchange, he dared—because it was a dare—to praise La Fontaine, in other words, to praise the logical, and that was very rare in poetry, since everybody preferred to be irresponsible and witty.

And here, I remember an epigram of Wilde, who said: 'If it were not for the classical forms of verse, we should be at the mercy of genius,' which is what happens now. Since everybody is considered witty, or, in other words, irresponsible.

Here, poets have come to see me, they have read me their poems, I have requested an explanation. They have said, no, they have told me that they write what occurs to them. Far from them the idea of responsibility, what they publish are first drafts—second drafts will not materialize. And that is very much admired. Moreover, they seek free verse because they erroneously believe that free verse is easier than the classical forms of verse, but exactly the contrary is what happens. If you do not take the precaution of being, well, Whitman or Carl Sandburg, what is called free verse is really bad prose typographically disposed as verse. However, it could be argued in favour of free verse that it's really careless prose or prose to which the author is resigned, that maybe it's convenient to print like verse because the reader knows that what he should expect from the page is emotion, and not information or reasoning. If he sees irregular lines, one over another, he already knows that this is done for emotion. On the other hand, if something is ordered like prose, he can think that this is done to convince him of something or to recount something, in other words, he has a narrative end or a polemical end. But if he sees the page with unequal lines, he thinks: 'Good, this must be read like a poem,' and, of course, we know that texts depend on the way they are read. So that, perhaps, that form can be justified.

Actually, no one begins with classical forms. When I say the classical forms are easier, people are astonished. Classical form gives one a scheme, even illusionary, of what one is going to do. For example, if you decide to write a sonnet, you already have a sonnet's plan. It can be two tercets or two quatrains, or three tercets and a distich. So, you have a plan, and later that can help you, although, really, a sonnet does not depend on those two possible plans which are always the same.

FERRARI. Of course, but we can't forget to recall that you called Valéry's 'The Graveyard by the Sea' 'a vast diamond'.

BORGES. I said it was a vast diamond?

FERRARI. Yes, you described the poem as a vast diamond . . .

BORGES. I would apply that word to other poems now, eh? I'd apply it to . . . well, it's evident what I'm going to say, but let's say, the *Orlando Furioso* of Ariosto. I think Valéry's poem isn't all that vast, and certainly it isn't so much a diamond, is it?, since it has some mediocre lines. How strange that nobody has compared 'The Graveyard by the Sea' with Gray's 'Elegy Written in a Country Churchyard'. They should have been compared, except that Gray seems to me superior. I think there is also an analogous poem by Hugo. We should look for that in his work. And it would be beautiful, it would be a lovely work to compare those three poems which are not alike but whose synthesis is or whose resumé would be very similar. And there would be room to signal the 'sympathies and differences' of Gray, Hugo and Valéry.

How strange that I wrote poems in the Recoleta and in the Chacarita—I don't know how I did, since now those places seem to me so horrible. I was in the Recoleta some time ago, by our vault— many of my elders are buried there—and I thought: If there is some place in the world in which my mother and my father are not, not to go any further, it is this vault. This vault, what it can contain—it is as if it contained, I don't know, hair cuttings, nail filings and horrible corruption. Well, that which Christ saw when he said that the Pharisees were whited sepulchres, in other words, beautiful outside and full of corruption within. And how strange that I wrote one of my first poems in the year 1923, a poem about La Recoleta. Later, in a book, entitled I think *Cuaderno San Martín*, there's a poem on La Chacarita, but I didn't find them horrible then. Now cemeteries seem horrible, and I hope not to be buried but burnt.

There's a very pretty poem, an Anglo-Saxon poem, 'The Sepulchre' whose theme is that—the theme is that death is so horrible it has to be hidden. And then, the theme about worms who divide themselves. And then it says . . . it compares the sepulchre with a house, it is a late poem, I think it's an eleventh-century poem, that is, later than the Norman conquest, perhaps the last poem written in Anglo-Saxon, or that we have from the Anglo-Saxon, and it says: 'That house has no doors and it is dark within.' And then it says to the dead man that when he is within, it is so horrible that no friend will come to visit him. That is to say, the theme about the atrocity of the corpse is a theme that has not been dealt with in general, has it?, well, there's like a decency of death.

FERRARI. It's avoided, yes.

BORGES. In Manrique's poem it is said: 'Our lives are rivers, which lead to the sea.' But nothing about that sad thing that we leave our body, condemned to corruption.

FERRARI. But, referring to death, you said that Valéry in 'The Grave-yard by the Sea' practised a speculation about death. He also wrote, you will recall 'The Young Park'. That speculation about death which is always attributed to Spanish poetry.

BORGES. I think so. Spanish poetry has the theme of death. Its prose has a theme, well, less poetic, which is the theme of hunger, isn't it?

FERRARI (*laughs*). That of the rogues.

BORGES. Yes, it seems that the protagonists are continually stealing cheese, for example. Those are the pranks.

16

'The Intruder'

●

OSVALDO FERRARI. Many times, Borges, we speak of Adrogué, and I think we ought to approach the following locality.

JORGE LUIS BORGES. Turdera. Of course, the payment of the Iberra, and of 'Sin barriga'.

FERRARI *(laughs).* And the scene of one of your stories, which I know you prefer, 'The Intruder'.

BORGES. Yes, 'La Intrusa'. Well, that story . . . I began with an abstract idea which doesn't augur anything good, the idea that the essential Argentinean passion is friendship. So when Eduardo Mallea published *History of an Argentinean Passion*, I thought: What Argentinean passion? Well, of course, there are others—avarice, for example—but what laudable Argentinean passion, if not friendship? But Mallea's book defrauded me in that sense, not in others. And I thought to write a story about that theme, in which it had to be noted that friendship in general is more important for us than love. And I recorded also the report of that old chieftain of Palermo, Don

Nicolás Paredes, who said that a man who thinks five consecutive minutes about a woman isn't a man—he is . . . and then a word derived from hermaphrodite which I can't here repeat.

So I thought I'm going to write a story about that: I'm going to show two men who prefer their friendship to the love of a woman. Now, as the concept of friendship has lately been contaminated, well, by sodomy, has it not? So no one can suspect that, I'm going to make those two men brothers. I'm going to seek fairly rough people. And I thought: What the hell! Too many of my stories take place in Palermo. I'm going to look for another quarter in which that kind of life, that type of cut-throat life went on for much longer than in Palermo. Then I thought of Turdera and I thought about the Ibarra brothers. And then I resolved the story of the two brothers—the two cut-throats. I gave them rather vague rustler's pasts, herders, gamblers, Caudillos' bodyguards. And I thought: A woman comes between them. And then the older of the brothers sees that their friendship is in danger, that there can be rivalry. He is the only character who speaks in the course of the story. And then he tries to arrange that by various methods. For example, he knows that he has that woman. His younger brother has fallen in love with her. And one night he goes off somewhere and leaves the other alone with the woman, and he says to the brother: There awaits so-and-so, use her if you want. And the brother does so. And afterwards, they go on sharing her. But she prefers the younger, and he becomes jealous. Then he sells her to a house of ill repute. Then the two meet in that house of ill repute in Morón, taking turns to be with her. Then they buy her, they take her again to their house in the outskirts of Turdera.

And there comes a moment when the older says to the younger that he has to carry some hides (they have a wagon and some oxen, given to them at the beginning of the story). And then they reach a piece of open ground, and there's a moment when he has to tell him—the older has to tell the younger—that he has killed the woman.

Now, when I arrived—I dictated that story to my mother for I had already lost my sight. When I reached that moment, I said: Well, the whole point of the story depends on this phrase. He has to tell him, and he has to tell him in few words so those words need to be sententious and efficacious. So I said to my mother: The older has to say to the younger that he has killed the woman, and the younger has to be an accomplice, to help bury her, to hide the body, et cetera. My mother looked at me, and after a short while, she said to me—with a very distinct voice: I already know what he said to him. 'I already know what he said to him'—as if that dream of mine had occurred and she had been present. She didn't say: I already know what he should say to him. No, she said: I already know what he said to him. That is to say, in that moment she accepted the reality of that vague dream of mine. Well, write it, I said to her. So she wrote it, and I said to her: Read it to me, and she read: 'To work, brother, this morning I killed her.' Now, that phrase is perfect.

FERRARI. It's perfect.

BORGES. First: 'To work, brother' means he is the older, and the other has to obey him. And then he says: 'this morning I killed her', so as not to enter into absurd details, such as yes I strangled her, yes I stabbed her . . . for what? 'I killed her'. Then the other resigns himself, and the two bury the body, and the story ends.

FERRARI. Between the two, everything was understood without saying. Including the crime.

BORGES. Yes, everything was understood without saying. Moreover, it was understood, well, that the most precious had been saved, that is, the friendship of the two brothers.

FERRARI. Certainly.

17

Oscar Wilde

●

OSVALDO FERRARI. There are two authors, Borges, both of Irish origin, with lasting influence, first in English literature and thereafter in all the literatures that you have periodically quoted.

JORGE LUIS BORGES. One would be Shaw, right?

FERRARI. One is George Bernard Shaw, and the other is Oscar Wilde.

BORGES. But we are forgetting Moore, we are forgetting Swift, we are forgetting Yeats.

FERRARI. It's just that in the time that we have, it would be very difficult . . .

BORGES. A small island with a slender population, six or seven million people, and it has given so many men of genius to the world. It's strange.

FERRARI. Truly.

BORGES. In exchange, you have very vast extensions that have given nothing, or almost nobody. And Ireland, well, starting with Johannes

Scotus Eriugena, a pantheist mystic in the ninth century in what should have seemed impossible, and was so, at the court of Charles the Bald. He could translate Greek texts while in France no one knew Greek. Even then, the Irish monks knew it. An extraordinary quantity of people of genius has Ireland given.

FERRARI. It seems to have given especially critical geniuses. Shaw and Wilde share that characteristic, don't they?

BORGES. Well, Shaw, of course, said that the English are sentimental and the Irishman easily incredulous and ironic.

FERRARI. Both had talent for the epigram, for the witty.

BORGES. We have forgotten another Irishman who Shaw used to remember, that is, the Duke of Wellington, Arthur Wellesley and another, finally, a minor author, Conan Doyle, born in Edinburgh but of an Irish family.

FERRARI. But perhaps Shaw and Wilde are those who have satirized English society most scathingly.

BORGES. Yes. I think the English like to be satirized. I think that, in some way, that is like a tribute they have paid to England. Another strange characteristic the English have is to choose, in each war, one of the enemies and see him as a hero. For example, in the First World War, it was the captain of the Emden, and some German aviator also. And in the Second World War, it was Rommel. Because England, if it's at war with a country, needs to admire someone in that country. It has that cult of heroes which it also extends to the enemy. And that doesn't happen in other countries.

FERRARI. What you say is very subtle.

BORGES. But it's easily observable.

FERRARI. Surely, yes.

BORGES. For example, Napoleon who, of course, was England's maximum enemy but who also had many supporters in England. When they told Byron, when they read of the victory at Waterloo, he said: 'I am damned sorry!'—he would have preferred a triumph of Napoleon over the English and the Germans. I remember a letter which Stevenson published, at the beginning of the war in South Africa, saying that the honour of England demanded they withdraw their troops, they had committed an error but that withdrawing the troops would correct it. This letter was published in the *Times*, yet it didn't give rise to any upset for Stevenson. They thought, well, he's saying what he thinks.

FERRARI. They are strangely capable of equanimity.

BORGES. Moreover, they try to be 'fair men', they try to be impartial. In other countries, no, it is considered that impartiality is like treason. I recall a letter, which was published by, I don't know if they were two officers, against some declaration of mine. This will have occurred a year ago. And in it I recall this curious article which said: 'This assertion, if made by a Chilean, would be all right, but in the case of Borges, who is Argentinean, no.' In other words, they admitted they weren't impartial, they admitted that a Chilean could give an opinion about a theme in a way different from an Argentinean, which seems to me absurd. It's that they don't seek impartiality either.

It was understood that an Argentinean has to give an opinion in such a way, and a Chilean in another way.

FERRARI. It's true, these flaws are given among us. We can also see that in England they bore a certain rancour towards Wilde, due to the criticism he made of English society and which was later used in evidence in the trial which sent him to prison.

BORGES. But he initiated that trial. because, according to Pearson, he lived in an illusory world. Good, we all live in an illusory world, but his world was the world of epigrams, of brilliant phrases. And he thought that could be extended, let's say, to others. That is to say, he knew that the accusation Queensberry had made against him was true but he thought he could defend himself by means of epigrams, by being more intelligent or clever than the judges—and that was his error. Now, why he initiated that campaign one doesn't know. It's said that he was led to it by Lord Alfred Douglas, the son, precisely, of the person whom he had accused of calumny.

FERRARI. Yes, but Queensberry was evidently offensive because he didn't only say sodomite but 'posed as a sodomite'. A gentleman like Wilde had to react.

BORGES. 'Posed as a sodomite' was, I think, Queensberry being astute. Clearly, because saying 'posed as a sodomite' was as if he said . . .

FERRARI. It aggravated him.

BORGES. No, he meant to say I am not sure he was a sodomite.

FERRARI. You think so?

BORGES. I believe it was a stroke of astuteness. If he had said 'to the sodomite', Wilde could have said 'no, I am not.' But 'posed as' shows a certain uncertainty. At the same time, the other was completely sure, since he had been followed to Paris by detectives and he had the certainty. But he pretended that uncertainty in order to encourage Wilde. I believe that he explains himself so, and to the point of not putting sodomite but 'somdomite', he makes a mistake in the word also but I think all that was deliberate.

FERRARI. Note that, in that trial, some of his university companions, for example, made statements against Wilde, people who had obviously hated him in secret from a long time before.

BORGES. But those who made statements were, above all, minors whom he had corrupted. What tricked him was that they were boys who were less than eighteen and whom he had taken to Paris. He had given them gold watches. Now he was not to know that all that was going to be made public. But all that embarrassing past of him appeared and, well, was enough to prove that it wasn't a calumny, that it was certain. Wilde had been able to leave England, since he had a month. And Frank Harris, Bernard Shaw and other friends had made him offers. They had told him to leave England, that he should go to Paris but he didn't want to, he stayed in England.

It seems that the last night he was alone, they heard him from below, coming and going in his flat. The chief of police sent a detective to the station where the last train left for Dover. The detective returned very remorseful and said: No, Wilde had not taken the last train. Hell, said the chief of police, we're going to have to arrest him. And they went and they took him. And he knew that was going to happen. Now, he explained later to Gide that he wanted to know 'the other side of the garden'. That is to say, he'd already known success, had known in some way glory, happiness, if happiness is possible, and he wanted to know also infamy, unhappiness. In other words, he wanted to exhaust the sum of human experiences, he meant that he deliberately sought it out.

FERRARI. And he did it with enormous nobility . . .

BORGES. With great nobility, and he made friends with the other prisoners and, later, when he left prison, he went on interesting himself in them, writing to them, helping them financially. He left prison and went to a lady's house, a Jewish lady. Then he went out with a friend and went, as is natural, to a bookshop. He was leafing through books and someone, whose name he never knew, said: Oscar Wilde is over there. Then he took account that, if he stayed in London, that was going to be his fate—in Ireland, it would have been much worse, of course. Then he went to Paris and died some years later.

FERRARI. How curious, about London he had said, in a passage in *Lady Windermere's Fan*: 'In London, one doesn't know if men make the fog or the fog makes the men.'

BORGES. It's good, that, yes. Good, here we have another way to flatter the English. They speak of the fog. They are proud of London's fog.

FERRARI. Now, you have said that it is verifiable that Wilde almost always was right, that is to say, that he is a man . . .

BORGES. I think that yes, I think that he thought deeply but that, through a kind of elegance, he wanted to be considered frivolous. Therefore he gave his judgements epigrammatic form.

FERRARI. Clearly.

BORGES. Now, as a poet, he's a mediocre poet, of course, a minimum Tennyson, a minimum Swinburne, but as a person, no.

FERRARI. And as a narrator he's wholly exceptional.

BORGES. Yes, but the style is very decorative. For example, you see *The Portrait of Dorian Gray* is copied from Stevenson's Jekyll and Hyde. *Dr Jekyll and Mr Hyde* is very well written, and *The Portrait of Dorian Gray* is not. It's full of padding, added chapters, long lists of musical instruments, in short, it's written in a decorative style.

FERRARI. But 'The Ballad of Reading Gaol' and the 'De Profundis' are all his, wholly Wilde.

BORGES. Yes, but 'The Ballad'—I don't know if it's good. Compared with a ballad like those of Coleridge or Kipling, it's nothing, or the authentic ballads of the people. No, it's all very false. For example, in the first verses he says that wine and blood are red. Now Kipling would have known, and doubtless Wilde knew, that an English soldier doesn't drink wine. The people who drink, drink gin. Not whisky either in that epoch. But wine is convenient for him, it has certain literary prestige. The riding jacket he used, it seems that being of a certain regiment it could not be red, it had to be green, and that some friend of his told him: The jackets are green. Good, said Wilde, if it seems to you better because blood and wine are green . . . (*laughs*) I'll put it, but they are better red. Clearly, he knew that was false. Later, allegories appear—they are equally false.

FERRARI. But I insist on that phrase, Borges, 'I shall convert my pain into music'. And I think that in 'The Ballad' and 'De Profundis', he achieves that in some way.

BORGES. I think so, and it's the function of every poet, I believe.

FERRARI. Yes.

BORGES. Clearly, to make music, to make cadences. Well, in the *Odyssey*, we read that the gods make men suffer so that the coming generations have something to sing. It is the same idea.

FERRARI. Certainly.

BORGES. It's to say that the whole universe would have an aesthetic justification, something Mallarmé said more prosaically: 'Everything for a book.' But a book is a dead thing. 'To have something to sing' sounds better, sounds much more alive. Homer said it with more skill . . . of course, Mallarmé said it with a certain resignation: 'Everything for a book.' As though he was saying: Good, we can hope, yes, everything for a book. Except he had the cult of the book, or there were both things, since Mallarmé was a very complex person. Possibly he would write in a deliberately ambiguous manner.

In the case of Wilde, I believe it undoubtedly, that further to each of his pages Wilde leaves us with the impression of a genial man and a charming man. Moreover, as I've said more than once, with a strange innocence, which also happens with Verlaine. In other words, their lives may have been infamous but they themselves were not. And this reminds me of a phrase of Stevenson, which is very pretty and which is true: 'A man,' said Stevenson 'may be slandered by his works, by his life, or by his acts.' That is to say, a man can kill and essentially not be an assassin. And the case of Macbeth would be that, wouldn't it? One senses that Macbeth works thus, impelled by the witches and by his wife who is stronger. He is not essentially an assassin. And it's that often an intelligent person can act like a fool. And he should not be judged by those stupid acts but by what he is. And, in the case of Wilde, the final impression he leaves is of a strange innocence, as if everything had passed to another or as if he had not participated at all in his life. Therefore it's a shame that they always insist on, well, Wilde's final tragedy. I should like to read some book about Wilde in which they do not speak about that, in which they speak, simply, about his work. But it seems not so, it seems at this time we have to talk about the trial, the prison, the years of unhappiness in Paris.

FERRARI. But you also say that the fundamental flavour of his work in happiness.

BORGES. Yes, I think so, I, without doubt, will have repeated that phrase; I think it is undeniable. Moreover, the fact also that in his comedies there are many silly people—society women, frivolous women—but they are also ingenious. But that doesn't matter, does it? The impression they leave is one of silliness, although they are continually saying ingenious things. Clearly, because Wilde puts those ingenious things in their mouths. They give a final impression of being silly, or of being frivolous, yet they speak in epigrams, in fortunate epigrams.

FERRARI. You tell me this now and I recall a phrase in Dostoyevsky in which, speaking of beauty, he says that beauty shines suddenly, including in stupidity.

BORGES. It's good, it's true. Yes, I, for example, in the street, sometimes hear extraordinary phrases said by persons who take no account of what they are saying. Now, Shaw said (since today we are with the Irish) that all his phrases were phrases he had heard in the street, that he had invented nothing—that he simply transcribed. But that can be one more of Shaw's sallies, can't it?

FERRARI. An amanuensis of the ingenuity of everybody else, yes, we have commented earlier.

BORGES. I don't believe that to be true. Moreover, how strange that nobody knows how to take advantage of that ingenuity except that casual hearer who is called, or who was called George Bernard Shaw. Well, Shaw and Wilde were great friends, and Shaw said that he would give anything for one or two hours of dialogue with Wilde, and that in that dialogue the one who would speak would be the other, and that he 'for once in my life,' he says, 'I should keep silent.'

FERRARI. In exchange, Wilde had said that he saw Shaw as a man incapable of passion and that, thought Wilde, would make his work of less interest for him: the work of Shaw for Wilde.

BORGES. Well, it's that Shaw had the passion of thinking, above all.

18

The Desert, the Plain

●

OSVALDO FERRARI. Periodically, Borges, we return to the plain, but this time with a new reflection. I have thought that the ambit in which one could suppose the great mystics were inspired should be much more the mountain than the plain. However, we have the concrete example of great monotheistic religions whose founders were inspired by the plain, by the desert.

JORGE LUIS BORGES. You are referring to Islam, and to Christianity, perhaps, or, no?

FERRARI. Yes, naturally.

BORGES. Yes, because I don't know what others it could be.

FERRARI. In those religions, the plain, in place of the mountain, has been the great inspirer. Now, you mentioned the perspective observed by Darwin of the flat lands of the plain.

BORGES. Yes, that is found in Darwin's *Voyage of the Beagle*, and is later picked up by Hudson, I don't know whether in *A Naturalist in La Plata* or in *Far Away and Long Ago*. Now, curiously, Francisco Luis Bernárdez said that title was the same as *Anos y leguas* by I don't know which Spanish writer. But it isn't, because *Anos y leguas* appears dry, doesn't it? I say, it speaks of time, and then it speaks of space. In exchange, *Far Away and Long Ago*, or even in the Castilian version *Allá lejos y hace tiempo* there is a cadence, like a music, which is equivalent . . . to nostalgia, a certain melancholy. I think that 'far away and long ago' figures in some ballad. That is to say, it says the same but it's said with a certain music, whereas *Anos y leguas* seems dry . . . the words are simply two ways of measuring time and space but without greater emotion. In 'far away and long ago' or in 'Hace mucho tiempo y muy lejos', there's a cadence which becomes a measure of emotion. So that they are not equal, I say. Conceptually they will be equal but emotionally, no. Intellectually they are equal, not emotionally.

FERRARI. But emotionally speaking, you said to me in another dialogue that perhaps the true manner of being in a place may be to be far away from it. Hudson wrote about those places from far away. And Güiraldes wrote about the plain from France, in other words, from far off.

BORGES. Good, partially. He wrote a part of *Don Segundo Sombra* at the ranch, in other words, on the plain, in the province of Buenos Aires, in San Antonio de Areco. Another part in Buenos Aires, partly in the house of his parents, on Paraguay and Florida, and another part in the house where he lived and where I visited him when he was writing that book, which would come to be Solís and Victoria, or Solís and Alsina, I don't remember. Anyway, in the Congreso quarter . . . once the plain but now no longer because it's built over.

FERRARI. In any case, distance acted as inspiration.

BORGES. Yes, I think so. We could exaggerate that and say that the only way to be emotionally in a place is not to be there physically, isn't that so?

FERRARI. Yes, I think you are right in this. There are other examples in our literature in which the work has been conceived at a distance. Particularly by works which refer to the plains, and in earlier epochs, in the last century.

BORGES. We have Sarmiento, who wrote the *Facundo* in Chile.

FERRARI. Exactly.

BORGES. Now, the case of Echeverría. Echeverría wrote his poem 'The Captive' . . . well, he wrote it on the plain, in a ranch in El Pilar. But he was thinking less about that ranch than the extension of the plain towards the Cordillera range.

FERRARI. Towards the Cordillera. Moreover he came from journeys around Europe.

BORGES. Also, it's true, yes, of course we remember Echeverría's guitar in Paris.

FERRARI. Then, we see that the plain poses different readings. But I come back to what you mentioned earlier, about Darwin, because there was a perspective which interested me. You told me the vision of the plain depended on the altitude from where one was looking.

BORGES. Yes, I think that Darwin, and later, Hudson, spoke about the plains on the plain, which became the plain seen from the height of a standing man, or from the height of the jockey seen from a horse, and he has to note that in no case does the view reach very far, because in both cases one very quickly reaches the line of the horizon. That is to say, that a person who is in the middle of the plain does not feel it as infinite. Except that he knows that virtually it is infinite but he feels it as greater, doesn't he? Because if the view doesn't reach very far, one arrives very quickly at the horizon which is a circle, and a circle which is not very far. On the other hand, the vision of the sea is greater because you see from the deck of a boat, then you reach much further than you see from a horse or yourself on foot.

FERRARI. There are three literary versions of the plain that have something to do with reality.

BORGES. Which are the three?

FERRARI. The one of Sarmiento, who says that in order to understand the Argentinian man, you have to know the influence on him of the natural medium. The one of Martínez, Estrada, who says that the pampas enters into us, into our cities, into our villages . . .

BORGES. Yes, and there's a phrase of Güiraldes, who says that before, the countryside entered the houses.

FERRARI. Oh, clearly.

BORGES. So that it becomes the same.

FERRARI. Exactly, it's the same idea.

BORGES. Yes. I don't know, it could be in some text of *The Crystal Cowbell*. Or in some of the poems after *Don Segundo Sombra* . . . I don't remember their titles. But in some of them he says something about the countryside entering houses.

FERRARI. And there is someone who reaches even further: Carmen Gándera, who says 'we the Argentinians are desert'.

BORGES. It's already installed within the desert. Yes, and it would be sad, and it could be true, eh? The fact that the individual feels alone. The community feeling is lacking. That is to say, a shared plain, right? We should be plain and we should be irreparably alone.

FERRARI. In some way, that isolation which we suffer from being people alone in the south, let's say, at the end of the world.

BORGES. Yes. I recall that Xul Solar said to me that it would be convenient if maps were printed in another way. Then, instead of being a kind of hanging rag, which becomes the austral cone, we should be at the peak, at the apex. Yes, we would be south, high up—not in the inferior part of the map.

FERRARI. Xul proposed to invert the map of the world, or the earth globe.

BORGES. Yes, but as he's dealing with only a convention, it would cost nothing: the same it could be, well, the south and the north the right and the left. Instead, now they are the inferior part and the superior part of the page.

FERRARI. Yes, the men of the plain who you have described in your stories, the characters are defined and even definitive. I'm thinking of a Tadeo Isidoro Cruz, I'm thinking of . . .

BORGES. Yes, it's true, that the character of people can be determined by cartography—but why not (*both laugh*), but perhaps not, perhaps this is more differentiated by the fact that they be mountain folk or plainsmen. Now, in dealing with the type of gaucho and, well, the type of gaucho is not only limited to the plain but also to the hills, where there are already elevations. But I don't know if that influences the character, does it?

FERRARI. Yes, apparently. There should be a difference made between people of the plain and mountain people of the same country. But, well, an agreeable difference of shades.

BORGES. Groussac, in the lecture about the gaucho that he gave in Chicago, I believe, says there are two types of gaucho: the southern type, which would be the plainsman, and then the type of gaucho in the mountain ranges, who came from the north. On the other hand, Lugones in *El payador* insists that the gaucho type is unique, and is so equally in a mountainous region like Salta, as in the plain. I don't know if that is true, possibly there are differences.

FERRARI. True, but I'm not thinking only of the gaucho, I'm thinking about ourselves as men of the plains also, since Buenos Aires, as we say when talking about the south is the built-up plain, let's say.

BORGES. Undoubtedly, I remember I was once conversing with . . . clearly, I was working with bad faith, I was conversing with a literate person, French I think, and he told me that he'd been staying in a hotel, I don't know, near the Plaza del Congreso. And he said to me he wanted to see the pampas. And I said to him: Well, we're already in the pampas, this is the pampas. But (*laughs*) it was a trick of mine, because what he wanted was not to see the built-over pampas but the desert pampas, let's say.

FERRARI. But there was another French literate who spoke, I think, about the pampas' horizontal vertigo.

BORGES. That was Drieu la Rochelle, but that was because we had set out to walk, and we reached, I don't know, the vicinity of the Puente Alsina or the La Paternal quarter, or wherever, somewhere in which one already felt the plain. And he said: *Vertige horizontal*. That was Pierre Drieu la Rochelle, on some lost morning, on the shores of Buenos Aires.

FERRARI. And it happened with you, Borges, Drieu la Rochelle was with you in that moment?

BORGES. We were Ibarra, Drieu la Rochelle and I. I don't think there was anyone else. The three of us had set out to walk and we arrived at the shores of Buenos Aires. I think we'd set out from San Juan y Boedo and we reached the Puente Alsina. But it could also have been the eastern side, although I think not, I think that it was, above all, the southeast, that is to say, the Puente Alsina. Yes, because I remember that . . . we saw a little troop. Yes, Ibarra reminded me about that, which I'd forgotten. And I said: The fatherland! and then a bad word, which wasn't a bad word but an emotional emphasis, you know?

FERRARI. But how curious, Borges, we were seeking a conclusion for this dialogue about the desert, the prairie, the plain . . .

BORGES. And the suicide has given us that phrase.

FERRARI. And the suicide, Drieu la Rochelle, with the horizontal vertigo, has given us the conclusion.

BORGES. Our friend has helped us, yes.

19

Adolfo Bioy Casares

●

OSVALDO FERRARI. From a literary point of view, Borges, you have maintained one friendship from which all of us have benefitted, since from that friendship books and important translations have arisen. I refer to your longstanding friendship with Adolfo Bioy Casares.

JORGE LUIS BORGES. Yes, I prologued his first book, *The Invention of Morel*. I remember that he put that title to record *The Island of Doctor Moreau* by Wells, and my sister drew a kind of plan of the island on the cover. I remember that island, yellow in a blue sea, and the prologue I wrote . . . because Ortega y Gasset said that our century could interest itself in arguments with difficulty and could not invent a new fable. Then, in a note published in the magazine *Sur*, I signalled precisely that this century had abounded in new arguments. I limited myself, I think, to the example of Wells—I spoke of Wells and I spoke of Chesterton, also of Kafka. And I said that our century was precisely characterized by the invention of arguments. And that one of them, and not the least beautiful, was that of the novel of Bioy

Casares. Now, I believe to write in collaboration was impossible but I went one Sunday to lunch at Bioy's house, and lunch was delayed for an hour, and he said to me: 'I'm going to write that story, whose argument occurred to you, and I propose to you that we write it in collaboration.' And I said yes, in order to demonstrate to him that collaboration was impossible. We started to write and, after a while, well, a personage took control of us who was called Bustos Domecq and, later, Suárez Lynch. He took control, and we began to write. I don't really know from what side of the table things surged. In general, I think the arguments were mine, and the phrases, the happy phrases, were by Bioy Casares. But I'm not sure about that, since some phrase will have occurred to me and some arguments to him, of course. Moreover, I think that to collaborate it is necessary for the collaborators to forget they are two persons, because if not, you can, through vanity, insist your opinion be accepted, or, through courtesy, that the other is always right. Whereas these things must be forgotten. It is necessary to judge what has been written, what is invented, in an impersonal manner. And we have achieved that with Bioy Casares. But, ultimately, we decided to abandon it to . . .

FERRARI. To Bustos Domecq.

BORGES. To Bustos Domecq and to Suárez Lynch, because, we don't much like what they wrote, and their baroque style displeases Bioy—Bioy has shown me the virtue of the simplicity of the classical—and now I, too, am displeased. However, as soon as we begin to write, that mystery surges, that ghost generated by our dialogue, and takes control not only of the argument but also of the phrases, and it tends towards the baroque, it makes a sort of *reductio ad absurdum* of what we are writing. In the end, it's some time since we collaborated.

FERRARI. And Don Isidro Parodi, does he come back sometimes?

BORGES. Yes, we chose the surname 'Parodi'. Curiously, and incredibly, we did not think about Parodi and 'parody'. No, we thought there are Italian surnames that do not sound Italian but like Creole. And I thought: Well, those surnames could be, for example, Ferry, that doesn't sound like Italian, Molinari, that doesn't sound like Italian, Parodi, that doesn't sound like Italian.

FERRARI. Clearly, certainly.

BORGES. Yes, and what's more, I remember a phrase of a friend of mine who said that all the old creoles were gringos, no? (*Both laugh*), that the old age of the gringo, in Buenos Aires, is that of the old Creole. And it's true.

FERRARI. Now, I emphasize the friendship of you two as beneficial and creative.

BORGES. But, of course. Always, when we are given a friendship between writers of very uneven age, it is supposed that the older is the master and the younger the disciple, but in our case it isn't so. The master has been the younger man, and the old disciple has been me. I wanted to emphasize this because it's a fact—one is not dealing, well, with playing with modesty, no, one is dealing with something that has happened—and that Bioy, without doubt, through courtesy, would deny, wouldn't he?, since it's understood that the older must be the master.

FERRARI. Good, but it's also certain that your attitude, Borges, is rather that of disciple in the face of things than that of master.

BORGES. Oh of course, yes, when people call me 'maestro', I look somewhere else . . . like when they say 'doctor' I think they are addressing a third party. Since I am used to calling myself Borges, and people call me Borges—people who don't know me call me Georgie, and the people who know me call me Borges, of course. Well, except my sister, naturally, she's not going to call me by my surname.

FERRARI. Of course. Bioy Casares and you have sometimes said that dealing with the two of you, one is treated to a friendship without intimacy. You have characterized a style of friendship that seems to me very special.

BORGES. Very real. In my case, I recall this type of friendship, above all, with Manuel Peyrou and with Mauel Mujica Lainez. Peyrou reached the extreme of getting married and communicating his marriage to me a little more than a year after having done so. Now, Peyrou was rather rare. He believed he had communicated his marriage to Silvina Ocampo because they spoke every day on the telephone, and one day he said to her: 'Well, yesterday I took a decision.' Now that phrase can be interpreted in many ways, but he thought he had told her that he had married. And then it turned out that he had told her in that way, at once sententious and enigmatic 'Yesterday I have taken a decision'—full stop. And he believed he had communicated to her his marriage.

FERRARI (*laughs*). It was well understood by him, in any case.

BORGES. Yes, it was well understood, supposedly. With Mujica Lainez as well, we have been very strong friends and we have seen each other perhaps . . . every two years. Above all, of course, I've spent a good part of my life in sanatoriums and they have done many operations on my sight, and always when they have operated there was Manuel Mujica Lainez. And I was out of the country when he died, so I received the news only on returning to Buenos Aires.

FERRARI. I've seen, Borges, that you have many friends whom you re-encounter over time. Recently, for example, you re-encountered Ricardo Constantino.

BORGES. It's true, it was very fine, he from Lomas, I from Adrogué, both of us 'southerners' . . . I hadn't seen him for a long time . . . he called me, I expect to see him again soon. He's an excellent person, wrongfully forgotten. Well, everything tends to be forgotten in this country, eh?, even dictatorships, even infamy, everything, everything is forgotten or forgiven, since to forget is to forgive and that apparently assures a certain impunity.

FERRARI. And sometimes we go from forgetfulness to confusion, isn't that so?

BORGES. And easily, forgetfulness is a confusion for the rest.

FERRARI. Now, in the case of Bioy Casares, you and he revised the magazine *Sur*, and revised the *Anthology of Fantastic Literature*?

BORGES. No, not *Sur*, I knew Bioy . . . Silvina Ocampo introduced me to him. She was not then his wife, she was a friend of my sister. No, it was not *Sur*. In any case, my relationship with *Sur* has been greatly exaggerated. I owe a great deal to Victoria Ocampo, but in the edition of *Sur*, no. I've published in the magazine occasionally, I figure in that editorial committee—which is a list of all the persons who were present when the Committee met, so that there appear persons who had nothing to do with literature. For example, I think Alfredo González Garaño is there, María Rosa Oliver is there, simply because they were present.

FERRARI. And they weren't consulted later?

BORGES. No, I don't think so—it's very difficult to consult Waldo Frank in New York, Ortega y Gasset in Madrid, Drieu la Rochelle in Paris, impossible. But it doesn't matter, it was like a gesture of salute to Victoria Ocampo.

FERRARI. A tutelary committee, let's say.

BORGES. Yes, yes, yes, tutelary rather (*laughs*), more tutelary now, since it's a ghost. But I believe the magazine has ceased, I'm not sure—does it go on appearing, or not? I think not, eh?

FERRARI. Neither am I completely sure, because the space between number and number is so great—we don't know.

BORGES. Yes, one easily reaches disappearance, passing through uncertainty. But it wasn't a periodical in the beginning, since Victoria's idea was to publish four numbers per year, which would correspond to the four seasons. But, of course, that didn't give any impression of periodicity, did it? A magazine that comes out every three months is more like a book.

FERRARI. It interests me, Borges, to emphasize the *Anthology of Fantastic Literature* done by you in collaboration with Bioy Casares and Silvina Ocampo.

BORGES. Well, I think that book has been an inestimable book, since the literature of South America, distinct from that of North America, has always been a literature more or less realist or *costumbrista*. Lugones, of course, published a book of fantastic stories and initiated the genre in South America. I refer to the *Las fuerzas estrañas*, naturally, the year, more or less 1905—my dates are unsafe—but it was the first book of fantastic stories, and he wrote it in the shadow of Edgar Allan Poe. But the books of Poe were in everybody's reach and not everybody wrote *Las fuerzas estrañas*. And above all, no one wrote stories like 'Isur', like 'The Horses of Abdera' and like 'The Rain of Fire', the best stories in that book. And there's an essay about cosmogony which becomes a variation of Poe's 'Eureka' which is also a cosmogony. Now Lugones entitled it—which is still funny, still odd— 'Cosmogony in Ten Lessons'. One doesn't associate the idea of lesson and that of cosmogony, does one? Cosmogony, I don't know, suggests something very ancient, while lessons, no, something didactic and actual. But that shows the composure of Lugones: he can teach cosmogony—which, according to Valéry is the most ancient of literary genres, he can teach it in ten lessons. Well, it's a bit of a trick which I repeated when I titled a book of mine *A Manual of Fantastic Zoology*. Fantastic zoology doesn't exist, even less a manual of that zoology. More or less the same trick, and I take that into account in this moment, conversing with you, Ferrari.

FERRARI. We see that Lugones didn't cultivate a sense of humour, but extravagance at times, yes.

BORGES. A sense of humour he cultivated but, let's say, with poor result. When he says, 'The governess, a skinny Scott / already entirely isosceles next to the obese mother-in-law', the intention was humour but the result was rather melancholic, no? (*Both laugh*)

FERRARI. Too harsh.

BORGES. 'Entirely isosceles' wants to be witty, but I don't know if it really provokes hilarity.

FERRARI. The other aspect of your work in collaboration with Bioy Casares is that of translation. I believe they have introduced important compositions, poems, above all from English.

BORGES. Ah, yes, there will be collaboration with Silvina Ocampo, without doubt in them, eh?

FERRARI. Also in the translations.

BORGES. I'm sure, yes.

FERRARI. As in the case of the *Anthology of Fantastic Literature.*

BORGES. Yes, in the case of the *Anthology*, of course. That anthology the three of us did, but it fell to Bioy to write the prologue. I think in that prologue he quotes, unabridged, the sonnet about a tiger by Enrique Banchs. The tiger is described at length, the autumn leaves are mentioned, finally, very unexpectedly—like in a police story or ghost story—in the last verse we find these last words: 'This is my hate.' Before he hasn't referred to hate, he has simply described the tiger. Bioy cites that as an example of surprise . . . I don't know if Banchs was capable of hatred, I think not. But perhaps he was, since he was a very reserved man . . .

FERRARI. It's a sentiment more conceivable in a tiger than in Banchs.

BORGES. The hatred in the tiger . . . no, I should say. Rather, rage, but an innocent rage, because hatred implies memory and perseverance. I suppose that animals, as Seneca observed, live in the present, that is to say, they live in the present and ignore death. I remember a very lovely line of Yeats who says 'Man has created death', in the sense that only man is conscious of death—animals are immortal since they live in the present.

20

Politics and Culture

●

OSVALDO FERRARI. On another occasion we have spoken, Borges, about culture and ethics. Particularly, about the importance of maintaining an ethical attitude in culture. And how you have been a witness of different manners and conceptions with which culture in our country has been managed. I want to consult you about these new forms which are massively given us in, for example, the Feria del Libro or the book fair.

JORGE LUIS BORGES. Examples abound. The fact of decreeing, for example, that this is the Gardelian year. That neologism has not made us draw back appalled. Furthermore, to dedicate the Feria del Libro to, well, to someone as far from the concept of the book as Gardel. These are demagogic methods, I think, aren't they? Somewhat rough but, contrary to what Gracián, the author of *El cortesano*, thought. I don't think it's convenient for shrewdness to be very shrewd. I think it's the contrary, I think it's convenient to have rough strategies, since the majority of people is rough. And something so evident as the fact of dedicating a year to Gardel is, well, somewhat rough. But it doesn't matter—it's effective precisely because it is rough. I think that the idea that subtlety is convenient is an error, treating it thus. The majority of people, no. It's convenient that the means be as rough as those to whom they are directed.

FERRARI. The rough is more accessible, shall we say?

BORGES. I think so, yes. So that a very subtle person is not convenient. He would become the opposite of, let's say, Machiavelli, no?, the contrary of Gracián—the idea of maximum sharpness. And I think that is an error. If one proceeds with rough deceits, they may deceive more easily, since they are directed at rough persons also. So that everything plays a game and the over-subtle maybe doesn't function, is useless maybe.

FERRARI. You know that, in earlier decades, one couldn't conceive a demonstration which gathered together, in fifteen days, a million people, as happened last year in the Feria del Libro.

BORGES. Ah, yes.

FERRARI. But, perhaps precisely because they manage to gather together a million persons, it's important how they manage, let's say, that vast cultural pretext.

BORGES. Yes, in this case it seems they have looked for demagogic ends.

FERRARI. Naturally, we're not in this case referring to the book. And you will remember that in earlier decades you said that books and writers were almost secret.

BORGES. Yes, and now, well, I'd say that a secret writer must be a kind of oxymoron. One understands that the writer has to be public, he has to be as public as politicians (*laughs*). And, above all, now that publicity is exaggerating itself. Doubtless, I have told you this many times: When we arrived in Switzerland in 1914, like good South Americans we asked the name of the president of the Swiss Confederation. They stood looking at us, because nobody knew it. There was a very efficient government, but it was an invisible government. Whereas now we are governed by persons who are continually exposed to photography. Not only are they exposed, they seek it out. Clearly, they travel not only with bodyguards and an entourage but also with numerous photographers. The contrary of Plotinus, do you recall? I believe the other day we mentioned they wanted to do a bust of Plotinus. And because Plotinus said that he was nothing more than a shadow, the shadow of his archetype, an image of him would be the shadow of a shadow. And that argument Pascal encountered several centuries later, against painting, saying that if the world is not admirable, why was the representation of the world going to be so, without knowing that he was repeating Plotinus.

FERRARI. That is very clear.

BORGES. Yes, but now I believe nobody thinks so. A person who is not portrayed almost doesn't exist, does he? (*Both laugh*) And the images are more real than the beings.

FERRARI. Than the realities.

BORGES. Than the realities, yes.

FERRARI. But you said that writers thought that the less multitudinous they were, the better quality their work.

BORGES. Yes, because there was the idea of the 'happy few'. There was the idea, in some verses of Stefan George, which I don't remember in German but which in a translation by Díez Canedo and referring itself to the poem goes thus: 'Rarely chosen / is rarely prize.' Well, that was the ideal of a poet. And I think it's a poem whose title is taken from a story by Henry James, 'The figure in the Carpet', which begins with a carpet whose drawing at first sight is a chaos of colours and forms, and then one, concentrating, sees that there is a secret symmetry. And Stefan George did a poem: 'The carpet of life' with that same idea that everything seemed chaos but that it really was a secret cosmos. And, then, that idea also for the work of art: 'Rarely chosen / is rarely prize', which becomes a little the idea of Góngora, or of Mallarmé. They are deliberately obscure poets because they do not write for ordinary people.

FERRARI. Of course, but that idea was not linked, as is usually believed, with elite culture and mass culture. It's got nothing to do with that.

BORGES. No, I think not. It's thought that every reader must try to be worthy of that apparent obscurity.

FERRARI. It's the idea that the poem finds its reader, or the painting its viewer, let's say.

BORGES. Yes. Moreover, there were commentaries which justified and explained the text. Recently that has happened with Joyce. That book by Stuart Gilbert, Joyce's secretary, and another, which is curiously called *A Picklock for Finnegan's Wake*, done by two North American students who dedicated five or six years, installing themselves in Dublin, to find the solutions to the topography and history of Dublin which are enclosed in *Finnegan's Wake*.

FERRARI. And thinking about Joyce, what's more.

BORGES. Thinking about Joyce, yes.

FERRARI. Now, culture understood as spectacle, instead of as silent spiritual manifestation, is proper to our epoch.

BORGES. Yes, it's understood that everything is spectacle. Clearly, spectacles can be lovely, of course, there is a beauty in spectacle also.

FERRARI. But it's obvious we are faced by a big change in cultural conception, in cultural manifestation.

BORGES. Oh yes. It's understood that things have to be spectacles, the mass is sought. Every man wants to be 'The man of the crowd' in Poe's famous story.

FERRARI. It's possible that this corresponds to a change of epoch, or to the inclusion of politics within culture.

BORGES. I rather fear it may be the second, eh? It's that politics, now, is ubiquitous, it seems.

FERRARI. Certainly.

BORGES. Above all, by the latest political opinion. The most obvious case would be Lugones who professed, perhaps, all political creeds but is remembered for the last. He is remembered for *The Hour of the Sword* which was the last, but not that before he was, well, anarchist, socialist, democrat, a supporter of the allies, that he saluted the

Russian revolution—good, that revolution promised fraternity to all men—and then finally, disillusioned, he believed in the creed of *The Hour of the Sword*. And he is remembered for that last, and it's forgotten that he did not prosper with any of those, well, let's say, transmigrations. He prospered with none of them.

FERRARI. Notice that before he didn't have the prestige and influence that he now has. Psychology, sociology, politics, for example. I'm referring to our country in this case.

BORGES. My father was a professor of psychology—well, the theme of psychology interested very few people. But I don't know if that is the psychology that is now studied.

FERRARI. Social psychology, in many cases.

BORGES. Social psychology, and then when it is applied to the individual, it insists, above all, on an obscene interpretation of things, doesn't it?; Freud, etcetera.

FERRARI. It would seem that one thinks less in terms of art, of literature and of spirit, than in those disciplines.

BORGES. Unfortunately, you are right.

FERRARI. And it could even be thought that, sometimes, what is wanted is to put culture and the spirit at the service of those disciplines which are peripheral.

BORGES. We don't even know if sociology exists or if it's an imaginary science. To judge by the results it has given, it doesn't exist. Because before, one didn't talk about economists but the country prospered. Now they almost don't speak about anything else and the result of those experts has been the ruin of the country. But that doesn't matter—it goes on being spoken about, that science goes on being insisted on, a science possibly no less imaginary than alchemy.

FERRARI. Certainly, the so-called social sciences are not sciences maybe. Sociology started with Auguste Comte.

BORGES. Yes, but up to now I don't know if it has produced anything.

FERRARI. Of course, we don't know if they have really converted themselves into sciences, or not. And they are studied under that label.

BORGES. It seems that the word 'science' is enough—that it's not important to know if it is a science.

FERRARI. Then, this big difference that we see in how it confronts culture. Before, let's say, silently . . .

BORGES. And efficiently. And now noisily and vainly. But above all noisily, that is what's important.

FERRARI. Yes, and that noise ends by involving all of us.

BORGES. Yes, not only to confuse us but also to drag us . . . to the abyss, let's say, using a rather easy metaphor.

FERRARI. But then, this association with which we have begun, that of ethics with culture, you recognize that it's very important for the destiny of culture in our country, in whichever case.

BORGES. Yes, but I think that each one of us will think of being an ethical man, and will try to be one. Already we have done a lot, since in the end the sum of conducts depends on each individual.

FERRARI. Exactly.

BORGES. sometimes I feel responsible for things. Although I know that, strictly, I am not, but in some way I am responsible. As victim or . . . as accomplice often, accomplice through laziness, through observing good manners . . . one has to resign oneself to many things.

FERRARI. A few years ago, you had returned from the United States, and you said you perceived amid the positive things among ourselves the capacity, the possibility of dialogue.

BORGES. Yes, dialogue is an art that has been lost in the United States. I recall that my friend Homero Guglielmini, who lived in Mar del Plata, said to me: 'It is a city without dialogue.' I thought: How sad that has to be. And Mastronardi said more or less the same to me, talking about Gualeguay. So what does one do in a little city? Well. One is reduced, like Alonso Quijano, to dialogue with the barber, with the priest, with the niece, with the housekeeper, in the best of cases with the graduate Sansón Carrasco. And it's natural that he should prefer to all that the madness of being Don Quixote. Since the boredom has to be borne as well. I say not only the reading of books of knight-errantry but also the fact that already one can no longer go on living in a place in La Mancha, whose name Cervantes does not want to remember. It's that the most intense part of Alonso Quijano's life has to have been his reading of those novels of knight-errantry.

FERRARI. Undoubtedly.

BORGES. All the rest has to have been very grey. The proof is that Cervantes tells us nothing of that, except that he was vaguely in love with a farmhand, Aldonza Lorenzo. And that's not very certain either for it seems she never took any notice. So that reading was the most intense moment of his life. And I sometimes think in that sense I am also Alonso Quijano, since reading has provided me with so much happiness. Now, unfortunately, well, I'm an Alonso Quijano exiled, since I'm surrounded by a library that leaves me very far behind.

FERRARI. Good, but you can read that library.

BORGES. But, of course, and I thank you greatly for what you have done.

FERRARI. I told you, finally, if you recognize that between us existed for a few years at least the capacity of dialogue, that . . .

BORGES. And possibly this is now getting lost, eh?

FERRARI. But that would indicate that we also have a certain form of cultural capacity which should be taken ethically, in order to be developed.

BORGES. Yes, but as we now live continually bombarded by television and radio . . . I should not speak badly about those media of communication, since we are going to use them, aren't we? But, why not?

FERRARI. You once said that it depended how they were used.

BORGES. Clearly, a means of communication in itself cannot be either good or bad. It's how it is said that writing is good or bad. But perhaps the imprint has been bad, since it has facilitated the multiplication of books—maybe there is already a sufficient number of books. Furthermore, now whichever book immediately receives publicity. In exchange, before, a manuscript copy was necessary. Then, people, before copying a text, hesitated. Now, no, now it is a question of a few days and they multiply, they centuplicate the copies. It becomes a public danger. And the National Library has to receive all that.

FERRARI (*laughs*). In every case, this noise, these slightly harmonic manifestations that we perceive in culture, will they have begun with printing?

BORGES. Yes, I have read about an Italian bibliophile who has a very well-cared-for library but he never allows a printed book. Now, I imagine the first printed books will have been singularly ugly. In exchange, manuscripts will have had the delicacies of calligraphy. The first printed books must have been very, very ugly, made in a rough way.

FERRARI. They will have been able to be perceived by means of that calligraphy you say, the human hand.

BORGES. Yes.

FERRARI. And not the machine, of course.

BORGES. In exchange, the first doubtless came from the machine, well, recently invented and rather crude.

21

Bernard Shaw

●

OSVALDO FERRARI. There are some lines of Shaw in that book which you and Bioy Casares compiled, Borges, I refer to the *Book of Heaven and Hell*, and I think that those few lines, differently from others we encounter, are not going to be, for us, incomprehensible.

JORGE LUIS BORGES. I didn't know there would be incomprehensible lines . . . Oh, of course, yes, those of St Thomas. Yes, I remember, yes, I have told them to several persons and they haven't been able to believe me, it seems to them impossible. I don't know with what intention that was written.

FERRARI. But this time we can demonstrate that the book is much clearer.

BORGES. But if it is judged by those lines . . .

FERRARI (*laughs*). It's lost.

BORGES. The book is lost, the labyrinth, yes . . . insurmountable.

FERRARI. Shaw says: 'I have been liberated from the bribery of Heaven . . . '

BORGES. Major Barbara says that about the Salvation Army. Yes, he doesn't say 'I have left behind the bribery of Heaven', that is to say, the idea of being awarded a prize for good actions, or, which comes to be the same, the fear of being punished for sins. It is that, yes, to be liberated from Heaven, clearly, because Heaven is, in fact, a bribe, and Hell is, in fact, a threat. I don't know which of the two is more unworthy of a divinity, do you? To threaten and to bribe seem very low operations ethically.

FERRARI. Shaw goes on to say: 'We carry out God's work by its very self; the work whose execution was created for us, because only living man and woman can execute it. When I die, let the debtor be God and not myself.'

BORGES. The last bit is very lovely, eh?

FERRARI. Very lovely.

BORGES. 'Let the debtor be God and not myself.' Moreover, that idea of giving something to the infinite divinity is a very beautiful idea. The idea of giving something to God, since everything is God's. Nevertheless, man can give him something.

FERRARI. Only he could have been capable of such an idea. It's really original.

BORGES. Yes, it's surprising, but it's much more than surprising. I think what no one can see in Shaw is his ethical nature. Shaw is always seen as witty, but he had to be seen as wise and as just. All that is forgotten, because it seems that his wit in some way has obscured the rest, has eclipsed the rest, hasn't it?

FERRARI. His interest in philosophy and the ethical.

BORGES. Yes, I think so. Furthermore, his invention of characters. You see, the personages of Shaw are really independent. Many don't think as Shaw does. Many are in complete disagreement with him, but one feels they were living persons for him.

FERRARI. Certainly, and of those personages, I think you have said that they exceed whichever personages imagined by the art of our time.

BORGES. You say the heroes, yes, because the novel has dedicated itself, above all, to human frailties. I'm thinking about great novelists, of Dostoyevsky, for example. He was interested in man's frailty . . . well, he had a romantic idea. You see in *Crime and Punishment*, the hero is an assassin, the heroine is a prostitute. All that would have been impossible in the case of Shaw. He had no romantic prejudice in favour of sin, but Dostoyevsky did, although he would have rejected that imputation. Precisely, in Dostoyevsky there is a kind of cult of evil. That one of the books was called *The Devils* demonstrates it. He liked the idea of evil. In the same way that Baudelaire liked it, and Byron was seduced by it. But in Shaw's case, no, Shaw is a lucid man, and, moreover, a great inventor of, well, of those illusory multitudes who compose literature.

FERRARI. In general, the vision of Shaw isn't religious—clearly, it's ethical and philosophical.

BORGES. But he could conceive religious persons because, without doubt, Major Barbara is in some way religious. Saint Joan, without any doubt, isn't she? And one believes in them. And it's very hard to create heroes or heroines thus, who may be virtuous and who may be real also. I think they were imagined with sincerity by Shaw. Doubtless, Shaw had a great soul. But, well, a generous soul and an extraordinary creative gift. And his work is . . . is fantastic. *Back to Methuselah*, for example, a kind of universal history which starts from Eden and then makes things return to God, like in the metaphysics of his fellow countryman Johannes Scotus Eriugena. The same idea that everything returns to God. Hugo also had that idea. There is a lovely poem by Hugo which is called 'Ce que dit la bouche d'ombre' and the mouth of the shadow says, with the vast metaphors we expect, and certainly obtain in the work of Hugo, a sample of that new cosmogony: the creation of the world and then, finally, all things return to God. And in the last act of *Back to Methuselah* also creation returns to the divinity, and one does not know what may happen after.

FERRARI. Yes, now, we have spoken earlier of the critical capacity of some Irishmen, but, in particular, the critical capacity that Shaw and Wilde had within England.

BORGES. It's that Ireland is an extraordinary country. Isn't it? A lateral little island, and yet it has given us so many men of genius. And all completely different from each other: What has Yeats to do with Shaw? I should say absolutely nothing, except the fact of both being geniuses. Or Oscar Wilde and George Moore, or Swift and Escoto Erígena. So many men of genius given by that lost little island.

FERRARI. The Duke of Wellington, I believe . . .

BORGES. The Duke of Wellington also, of course. He was sceptical about what concerned war, since he would not permit the history of the battle of Waterloo to be written, because the memory of the battlefield horrified him.

FERRARI. Now, I had mentioned to you earlier that Wilde considered Shaw a man incapable of passion.

BORGES. No, I don't think so.

FERRARI. And he, Wilde, thought that Shaw's work was going to interest him less because of that, exactly.

BORGES. The two were intimate friends, and Shaw tried to defend him but he could find nobody. Because they were looking for Sarah Bernhardt to sign, I don't know some text, and she was in London, and she said, no, that she was a foreigner and could not intervene. In fact she did not want to sign. There were two persons ready to help Wilde—one, Frank Harris, a somewhat subaltern being, and the other, Shaw. And, it seems, nobody else.

FERRARI. Yes, now, you told me that Shaw's passion was to think.

BORGES. Yes, in that book *Who's Who*, where persons have to list their pastimes, he put 'to think'.

FERRARI. That is proof indeed. And then, we have the other aspect, Shaw's political position. I believe Shaw adhered to socialism.

BORGES. He was one of the founders of the Fabian Society. And he thought it was necessary to delay the revolution, he thought that governments would collapse on their own, that a revolution would not be necessary. However, we are in the year 1985, and it seems that governments have never suffered so much as now, isn't that so? Never have they been so oppressive and so, let's say, omnipresent, incessant. One cannot take a step without the government now. However, in the nineteenth century, it was possible to believe that no, that governments were spending themselves, were tiring. Now nobody expects that.

FERRARI. Nobody. Moreover, he said that possibly the revolution would be made by the rich.

BORGES. Yes, because he thought that capitalism exposed two evils: to the poor, of course, misery, and to the rich boredom. And that of those two evils, it was perhaps easier to tolerate misery than to endure boredom. So that the rich will make the revolution. Something that for the moment does not seem probable, does it? We now have so greedy a world. But perhaps it may be unjust to judge countries by their governments. For example, I think one of the evils of this epoch is nationalism. But the people, unless one asks them an opinion, a person is more or less ready to read a book of whatever country, of whatever epoch, he is not continually closing himself. But governments are. The office of them is to insist on limits. But the people, no. If a film has a success in New York, it has success . . . and doubtless in Buenos Aires, doubtless in London and, if they allow it, doubtless in Moscow also. It seems to me that governments, compared with their countries, correspond to epochs obsolete or backward. The classic example would be, let's say, what was called Nazism, an invention of Fichte and Carlyle. It never had a revolution in that epoch, but in this epoch it did—we have had Hitler and Mussolini who are, in some way, well, caricatures of the heroes who Carlyle yearned for. When we think of political history, what is happening now is something that corresponds, without doubt, to dreams which almost nobody dreams except for politicians. (*Both laugh*)

FERRARI. I believe that the reminder of Shaw has inspired Borges, hasn't it? The other aspect, which seems to me very lovely in Shaw, is that he had said, regarding his phrases, that they were phrases he had heard in the streets, that they were phrases said by others.

BORGES. Yes, it's a form of his modesty. But very often one hears memorable phrases in the street. Good, we have already spoken of that also, the fact that intelligence, beauty, happiness are not infrequent—they are continually lying in wait for us. What we are dealing with is to be sensible to them.

On Film Criticism

●

OSVALDO FERRARI. I have taken the opportunity of getting to know in a volume published by *Sur*, your notes, Borges, about films which were premiered in Buenos Aires between 1931 and 1944.

JORGE LUIS BORGES. Well, I wrote much more, but the compiler, whom I do not know, did not examine two magazines, one directed by Carlos Vega and the other by Sigfrido Radaelli. In those I published many notes, while in *Sur* only occasionally. But, I don't know why, they only reprinted those from *Sur* and the others remained relegated to oblivion which they doubtless merited.

FERRARI. But there it is proved that you had a very complete knowledge of the cinema of that time.

BORGES. I went at least twice a week. And I remember that when sound cinema began, all of us thought it was a pity, because immediately films were replaced by opera, and persons, well, happily forgotten, such as Jeanette MacDonald and Maurice Chevallier, took the place of earlier great actors. Everybody thought: What a pity.

The cinema, which had reached a sort of perfection with Joseph von Sternberg, with Stroheim, with King Vidor—and all that was lost with the opera. Yes, it was a real shame.

FERRARI. Now, you had the habit of commenting on more than one film in a single notice. For example, in the same review you commented on *The Assassin Karamazov*, a German film, with Chaplin's *City Lights* and Von Sternberg's *Morocco*.

BORGES. Ah, I didn't know that, but it may have happened. Of course, I had to fill a certain space. What's more, I'd write those reviews the day after having seen the film—when one has seen a film, one is keen to talk about it.

FERRARI. To comment on it, obviously.

BORGES. Yes. Without doubt, I took advantage of that in order to write about the films after having commented with friends. I don't remember what I will have said then, possibly now I would not be in accord with what I said. For example, I wrote a completely unworthy commentary of an excellent film—*Citizen Kane* by Orson Welles. I wrote that adverse review, I don't know why, a whim. I enjoyed complete freedom, because in *Sur* there was that, one could write what one wanted . . . well, of course, Victoria Ocampo directed the magazine, but she didn't censor. Even José Bianco, or before him Carlos Reyles, left us in complete freedom.

FERRARI. In another note you commented on King Vidor's *The Street*, and made mention of Russian films, such as Eisenstein's *October* . . . *Ivan the Terrible* . . .

BORGES. Yes, I remember *October*. About Ivan the Terrible: there were two versions. It's clear they followed the ups and down of politics. At first, they spoke badly about the tsars . . . of course, the Revolution, but later with the force of the Revolution, well, it was confused with power and with Russia's past. It was simply the government, then. There were two films about Ivan the Terrible, one unfavourable and the other favourable. Curiously, they were both directed by Eisenstein who lent himself to those ups and downs of government and who made good films, but all different.

FERRARI. Along with those, Borges, *The Battleship Potemkin*.

BORGES. Yes, but I noted that it was very improbable, didn't I?

FERRARI. Yes.

BORGES. Of course, because I remember that, well, the crew rebel, they throw the officers into the sea, and that is treated as a comic episode, since the officers are duly ridiculous, one has a monocle, another has glasses—in short, they have asked for it. And then they bombard the city of Odessa, and the only loss of life is a column with a statue. They don't kill anybody because, naturally, one is dealing with a good revolutionary cruiser and it can't show itself killing anybody, can it? Nevertheless, that was celebrated as a realist film, which clearly is false. Moreover, that defect of Russian films, in which nuances are forbidden. For example, there are good persons and bad persons, and all the good are on one side, and all the bad on the other. It is made for fairly primitive people, no? At the same time, they were very interested in the photography, in that visually it was a very beautiful film. But there were no characters of any kind—everything was very simple.

FERRARI. You referred with great ability and precision, let's say, to the work of the actors and to the photography.

BORGES. Good, because the important thing was that. The rest was very primitive. Clearly that may have happened in the westerns also: the good on one side and the bad on the other, no? But, in the end, in American films, there is always generosity. In exchange, over there—no. For example, the films about the war—all the good is on one side, and all the bad is on the other. There is no generosity, no impartiality either.

FERRARI. Although they seem incredible, I found complimentary commentaries you made about Argentinian films (*laughs*).

BORGES. One by Luis Saslavsky, I believe?

FERRARI. Truly, *The Flight* by Luis Saslavsky.

BORGES. I think I ponder in it about the absence of local colour, because there was a scene in the ranch, well, they told us it was a ranch but they had spared themselves any country scenes. Above all, spectacular scenes, like breaking in horses. There was nothing of that.

FERRARI. The other is *Prisoners of Land* by Mario Soffici.

BORGES. . . . I think that was directed by Ulises Petit de Murat, wasn't it?

FERRARI. I believe he intervened . . .

BORGES. Or he had something to do with it, yes, well, we were friends, and possibly friendship . . . (*laughs*)

FERRARI (*laughs*). However, of this last film, you say that it is superior to the many our resigned republic has engendered and applauded.

BORGES. I said that? Clearly, I judged adjectives then. It's that 'resigned' is a good epithet for this republic, isn't it? Because if I have said 'submissive' . . . no, but 'resigned' is better. Something typically Argentinean the fact of resigning oneself. . . to whatever government above all, no? Yes, the cult of power . . . but that resignation is called 'native wit and cunning'. Of course, to the exercise of that resignation, we say: No, so-and-so is alive, because for him it's convenient to work in such a way. But, really, that can be cowardice. In the majority of cases it is.

Now, I don't know if I had any right to say such things, since I almost had not seen any Argentinean films. At that time, no one wanted to see national films. They told me that in France, for a long time, people did not want to see French films. They saw them from a sense of duty, but it was understood that the Americans were more entertaining.

FERRARI. In the cinema, one wanted to see other worlds, different from that in which one lived, surely.

BORGES. That could be, yes.

FERRARI. At the same time, the one who gathered these notes and wrote about you and the cinema in this volume of *Sur* was called Edgardo Cozarinsky.

BORGES. Oh, Cozarinsky, yes. I asked him why it hadn't been taken into account while preparing that list what I had published in Radaelli's magazine, and in the one of Carlos Vega, and he told me he didn't know about them.

FERRARI. He holds, in an introduction to the book called *Partial Magic of the Story* . . .

BORGES. Of course, that is taken from 'Partial Magic of the Quixote', that article of mine about the small magical touches there are in the apparently realistic world of Don Quixote. However, a note, well . . . they are brief magical touches.

FERRARI. Cozarinsky maintains in that introduction that the real condition of your essays is that of narrative exercises.

BORGES. Oh, it may be. It's true I wrote *A Universal History of Infamy*, in which I was going to get closer, cautiously and frightened, to the narrative, to the story, yes. Possibly there also I was trying to tell and didn't dare, since I . . . I so much liked stories! Especially those of Kipling, Stevenson, Chesterton. I thought I was unworthy of tackling that genre—for many years—and then I did it in an indirect manner.

FERRARI. Through the essay.

BORGES. Yes. For example, in *A Universal History of Infamy*, I pretended what I was saying was historic but, really, it was falsified and modified, continually deforming. But Cozarinsky had taken account of that, then?

FERRARI. Yes, and he added . . .

BORGES. What has Cozarinsky done?

FERRARI. I don't know, but he says that you don't discriminate between fiction and non-fiction.

BORGES. Of course, because I was using the non-fiction for fiction.

FERRARI. Clearly, he got it right.

BORGES. Yes, but without giving me account of everything. In other words, he has been more perceptive than I.

FERRARI. Well, he gives us an example—'The Wall and the Books'.

BORGES. Good, 'The Wall and the Books' is an essay . . . no, but I believe that everything is more or less true, although who knows.

FERRARI. Many conjectures are made . . .

BORGES. Well, but those conjectures become traps, but, I think, licit traps. How strange, I don't know that book.

FERRARI. It's called *Borges and Cinema*.

BORGES. Oh! I didn't know. If he had talked to me, I would have told him that he should forget *Sur* where I published very little about cinema, and that he should refer to the magazine *Megáfono* (horrible title) of Radaelli, and to that other magazine, that of Carlos Vega, who was a music critic or a musicologist. I took Vega to Paredes' house, and Paredes played some milongas, which he didn't know, which bore the name of . . . of forgotten singers. It seemed very lovely, the fact that a piece of music should survive.

FERRARI. I observe, Borges, that when you speak of what you would do if your sight were restored, you immediately mention books but not the cinema.

BORGES. It's that, after all, I don't think there is any film comparable to the *Encyclopaedia Britannica*, of the *Encyclopaedia Brockhaus*, of the *Enciclopedia Europea Garzanti*, is there? I don't believe there are any histories comparable to the history of philosophy.

FERRARI. However, you seem to have experienced a real interest in the cinema.

BORGES. Yes, I liked it very much. I went two or three times a week . . . that was linked to the remembrance of my friends . . . it's linked to the memory of Manuel Peyrou, of Haydée Lange . . . .

FERRARI. And of Bioy Casares.

BORGES. It's true, I think we have gone several times with Silvina Ocampo. I had forgotten that. Well, my parents also greatly liked the cinema. I remember that once we went to the cinema with them and with Carlos Mastronardi, and that there was a pianist in the cinema—it was the silent cinema, there were pianists who more or less followed the action. But the function hadn't begun, and they played 'El entrerriano' (The Man from Entre Rios). Then Mastronardi, who was an entrerriano, looked at my father, also an entrerriano, and said to him: 'They have recognized us, doctor.'

23

A New Conversation about Paul Groussac

●

OSVALDO FERRARI. When we spoke about Paul Groussac earlier, Borges, I told you I had the impression that you see him fundamentally as a stylist.

JORGE LUIS BORGES. Yes, I think the most important point about Groussac is style. But one could say that about Reyes, too. One means to say that beyond what he said, using that style as an instrument, is that style itself—and to create a style is no small thing. Moreover, he was a master of everything. He took as model the French language. He thought, I think with good reason, that Spanish, that Castilian, had not been worked like French, or that it had been worked in an erroneous manner. So he took French as a point of departure. And he thought that if Castilian reached the same economy, the same elegance and the same sobriety, it would have greatly advanced. And it is, in fact, what happened, beyond what writers may—or may not—have read in Goussac. It's undeniable that one of the maximum movements of Spanish literature was modernism. And as Max Henríquez Ureña observes and notes in his *Brief History of Modernism*, that movement which later inspired great poets in Spain came from this side of the Atlantic. Since those big names, let's say Rubén Darío, whom Lugones called his master, let's say Leopoldo Lugones, Jaimes Freyre, well, we could nominate many others . . . all were writing here in America, and that inspired great poets in Spain.

I remember having a conversation with one of the top Spanish poets, with Juan Ramón Jiménez, and he spoke to me of the amazement he felt when he read the book *The Mountains of Gold* by Lugones, published in 1897. When he showed that book to his friends they were astonished too. And then Juan Ramón Jiménez became . . . perhaps a poet superior to Lugones, but that has nothing to do with it, because Lugones was one of his stimulants.

Now, it will be said that modernism is nothing but an imitation of Verlaine and Hugo. But to bring the music of one idiom to another is very difficult, and the Castilian prose of Groussac is excellent French prose, written in an idiom which had not been submitted to that experience before. Now, if you have to choose some book by Groussac—well, I have selected one for a collection I'm now going to direct—that book is *Literary Criticism*. It begins with two admirable lectures about Cervantes—the best of what I have read about Cervantes. Moreover, in the whole of that book as a general rule, it dispenses with hyperbole, affirmation. Rather, it discusses the book. One of the dangers of Castilian is that the Castilian idiom leads easily to tribute. But not in the case of Groussac. In him. Castilian is an instrument of precision. And he worked hard. Groussac's fate is rare, because Groussac wanted to be a writer famous in France. However, his destiny was other—his destiny was to teach French sobriety . . .

FERRARI. In the Río de la Plata.

BORGES. And in the whole of South America, since one of his disciples was Reyes, one of the maximum writers of America. Clearly, Groussac could write then 'To be famous in South America is not to stop being an unknown.' And that was true when he said it—not now. Now a South American writer can be famous, but that did not occur then. So that Groussac felt defrauded, but he did not know that he fulfilled another destiny, which was to be, shall we say, a missionary for French culture here. And it's undoubtable that French culture has exercised a beneficial influence upon us. And then, having exercised it here, it has also exercised it in Spain, because although geographically Spain is alongside France, it is much further from France than us, much further than South America.

Now, it's a pity that the study of French culture has been left here. Because it's said that French has been replaced by English, but that is false. French was studied precisely to be able to enjoy the French language. English, on the other hand, is not studied to enjoy De Quincey or Shakespeare or whosoever—it is studied for commercial ends. It's completely different. Groussac was also an excellent historian. I wanted to record here his biography of Liniers, an admirable book, and then the essays in *The Intellectual Journey*. The title is not very happy, but the book is, which is more important, and the essays about Argentinian history. All that is not only an easy but also a gratifying read. And that is one epoch in which the Spanish idiom spread in a baroque manner, in other words, in a vain manner. But Groussac didn't write conceitedly—he wrote with precision, and with irony.

FERRARI. Was it possibly that idea of his, of French as a model, which made him deny North American literature of the last century, for example?

BORGES. If not, it is not explained in another way. Because he had the Shakespeare cult, maybe inherited from Hugo. For him, Shakespeare was the maximum writer. I recall an excellent study of his, precisely in *Literary Criticism*, about Shakespeare's *Tempest*, and then another about Francis Bacon. All that Groussac judged very, very well. His books are read with a great deal of pleasure. I've observed that, at least in this country, the taste for Spanish literature is an acquired taste: Spanish literature costs all of us some work. On the other hand, French literature: no—it arrives easily. The Italian and English also. But, above all, the French. In exchange, Spanish costs some work.

Now I spoke about that with Reyes, and Reyes told me the reason was this: when one reads a book in French, one thinks it is a book written in another idiom, by persons from another atmosphere, and one expects there to be differences. In the case of a Spanish book, as the idiom is the same, one notes, above all, the differences and those differences shock. Reyes said to me: What happens with Spanish literature is that it costs us to admit the different and the same. In exchange, if we expect something completely different, and we find it is not so different but that it's very close, and that it's free, moreover, then, well, we are grateful for that.

FERRARI. In that book, in which you selected part of the work of Groussac, you chose also from *Literary Criticism, From the Plata to the Niagara* and *The Intellectual Journey*.

BORGES. Yes, those would be the books.

FERRARI. That you preferred by him.

BORGES. Yes, there was also a polemic, but he suppressed that polemic. A polemic . . . yes, there was a polemic with Menéndez y Pelayo about what was called 'The False Quixote'. I think that although Groussac wasn't right in that polemic, well, he was right in . . . he attributed that book to an author and later it turns out it's not so, but the more important thing isn't that, it's all about the study of the Quixote and about the fact . . . Groussac was one of the first who pointed it out, and then Lugones pointed it out later, that the least important aspect of the Quixote is the style. That is what is usually imitated, and the importance is the invention of the personage, that personage who is ridiculous *and* lovable, Alonso Quijano. And Groussac noted that, and that, for example, well, in the case of Unamuno, for him, Don Quixote is an ethically exemplary personage.

FERRARI. Certainly. Now, as we have previously recorded, according to you, Groussac was humanmist, historian, Hispanist, critic, traveller and, moreover, a civilizing influence.

BORGES. Yes, a civilizing influence, of course. And he had to have influenced Lugones also. Although Lugones didn't wish to recognize him later. I believe that the influence of Groussac is a beneficial influence, and he goes on exercising it still. That is to say, actually that influence is so general that it's not necessary to have read Groussac.

FERRARI. Oh, clearly.

BORGES. Because he has arrived through his disciples.

FERRARI. He is disseminated.

BORGES. Yes, that is what happens with really important books, that in some way they get to be, well, part of the general consciousness. So that it doesn't matter not to have read them.

FERRARI. Yes, and finally, we have to record that you coincide with the National Library. Well, 'coincide' is a way of speaking with the passage of time.

BORGES. Yes, our destinies in some way are similar. I wrote a poem about that, but I didn't know when I wrote it, that we were not dealing only with Groussac and me but that there was another director of the National Library also blind.

FERRARI. José Mármol.

BORGES. Yes, José Mármol. So I did not know there had to be that sad and triple dynasty, did I?, of blind directors of the library. But it was convenient for me, because I should not have been able to manage three characters in a poem. In exchange, with Groussac and myself I could do it. But if there had been a trinity—it would have been impossible. For literary reasons, that trinity would have been rather inexplicable. So that, happily for me, I ignored Mármol when I wrote the poem.

FERRARI. You did not know that.

BORGES. No, and according to some it is one of my better poems: 'The Poem of the Gifts', and the theme is, well, that blindness can also be a gift.

FERRARI. Yes . . .

BORGES. And I have thought that, and that, doubtless, Groussac will also have thought, and in the same place. In other words, in some manner, for an instant even, I have been Groussac, and I must be grateful to that destiny.

FERRARI. It is: 'No one reduces the tear or the reproach.'

BORGES. Exactly, yes. That is to say, for some moments, I have been Groussac, since he has thought the same, has felt the same environment. And, doubtless, at the same desk. And to have been Groussac, even though it be for a moment, is something that one must be grateful for, or I must be grateful for.

FERRARI. And Groussac was Borges also.

BORGES. Good. I don't know if it was gratifying for him.

FERRARI. I think it was.

BORGES. I don't know if he noticed me. My grandfather, yes, because he mentioned him. In a text he says: 'Borges'. And then in a note he says: 'Borges, Colonel Francisco'. So evidently, he is referring to my grandfather. If I had not known Groussac, at least my name had sounded to him clearly. 'Borges' had been said, and that would not have been an empty word. He would have been reminded of my grandfather who was killed during the surrender of Mitre in the Battle of La Verde in 1874.

FERRARI. As you have recorded on another occasion.

BORGES. Yes. Actually I feel very far from my grandfather, but I try to feel myself—and it costs me nothing—I try to feel close to Groussac, since for me Groussac, well, he is a person much more alive and more detailed than my grandfather.

FERRARI. And what's more, it cannot be chance having coincided in the library.

BORGES. I don't know. I aspired to be director of the Library Lomas in Zamora but I failed (*laughs*). But, equally, it fell to me to be director of a library in the south. In the Monserrat quarter but not in Lomas.

FERRARI. Failed in the Antonio Mentruyt Library but not in the National Library.

BORGES. Ah, it's called Antonio Mentruyt?

FERRARI. Yes.

BORGES. Good, I aspired to that, and I confided that hope to Victoria Ocampo who told me not to be an idiot.

FERRARI (*laughs*). Who chose the National Library.

BORGES (*laughs*). Yes, effectively.

24

Letters in Danger

●

OSVALDO FERRARI. I've read in a Buenos Aires daily, Borges, a letter of yours whose title is 'Culture in Danger'.

JORGE LUIS BORGES. Yes, but I wanted to change that title, because 'culture in danger' doesn't sound right. I'd thought to put 'letters in danger' to avoid elision, but perhaps people are more interested in culture, even nominally, than in letters, which are a theme, well, especial—letters are included in culture, and not vice versa. So that we keep that title, a bit cacophonous: 'The culture in danger'—since the word culture is an unpleasant word, but it's the only one, isn't it? And it is the just word beyond its pleasant or unpleasant connotations.

FERRARI. If you accept, I should read your letter, so that you can explain what it deals with.

BORGES. Well why not.

FERRARI. 'It's rare that somebody wants to have been the subject of a joke; improbably, such is my case. A manuscript has reached my hands whose matter is the reform—as it calls it—of the studies of the Faculty of Letters of the University of Buenos Aires. I am a doctor emeritus of that house' . . .

BORGES. I want to explain a little my actions: I taught some twenty years—we choose round figures—not English or North American literature, which are infinite, but, yes, the love of those literatures, or, more concretely, the love of some writers. Sufficient that a student fell in love with an author and searched for his books, for me to feel justified. I don't know if I told you that some time ago I was detained by someone in San Martín Street, a stranger who said to me: 'Borges, I want to thank you for something.' And I said to him: 'What do you want to thank me for, señor?' And he said: 'You made me know Robert Louis Stevenson.' For that alone, I told him, I felt justified. I felt very happy because to have made someone know Stevenson is to have given him . . . to have added a happiness to his life. So that I have taught love, not of all those literatures, since I failed with many books of those distinguished literatures, but, yes, the love of some books and of some authors, or, why not, of even one author. For my task, that is already enough. The rest, well, is proper for encyclopaedias, for histories of literature . . . names, dates, all that is secondary.

FERRARI. You add, then: 'In this occasion, as in others, I have not been consulted' . . .

BORGES. Of course, I'm going to tell you why I put that. They nominated José Luis Romero and myself as professors emeritus. So I asked Romero: 'What does that emeritus mean?' He said: 'Really, I don't know, I suppose it means to say consultative.' But I've never been consulted, so his explanation was not to the point. Perhaps he was dealing with a mere complimentary sound, simply verbal flattery. They gave me that antepenultimate word 'emeritus', no? And why not thank the proparoxytones, one of the virtues of Castilian which other idioms don't have? Very well, I'm a professor emeritus although I don't know what that means. I thought it wanted to say retired, but apparently not. It seems, moreover, that it has a complimentary connotation, doesn't it? Because 'pensioner', 'retired', appear a little fixed on a course, but 'emeritus' seems . . .

FERRARI. More laudable.

BORGES. Yes, more laudable. Also less melancholic, isn't it? Well, let's continue.

FERRARI. Then you said: 'I have not been consulted, but I believe with right to give opinion', and I transcribe the text that they have told you is in circulation.

BORGES. They told me later that text is an exact text, and, extraordinary as it seems, this theme is going to be discussed in the same university.

FERRARI. The text is the following: 'All foreign literatures will be optional' . . .

BORGES. Well, optional means that you can leave it on one side, doesn't it? the word optional means that, yes.

FERRARI. 'And they can substitute, for example, by literature average and popular . . . '

BORGES. Well, here I confess my ignorance, above all, for what is average literature? Later I say it may be 'mediocre', but they have said to me, no, that one is dealing with bestsellers, in other words, something not usually appearing as literature. In any case, it excludes all that it may have as pedantry in the word literature, since the words 'average literature' make it more accessible, less alarming than 'literature' which can be very solemn.

FERRARI. I continue to read: 'They can be substituted by means of communication' . . .

BORGES. When I read that, I think of buses, diligences, trams, railways. No, they explain to me, one is dealing with periodicals, with magazines—which become small anthologies—or with radio, even radiotelephony. Now, it seems very strange that literature can be replaced by radio, but it appears that everything is astonishing.

FERRARI. Then it says: 'They can be substituted by literary folklore.'

BORGES. I think that I'll express an opinion about that later, but what can folklore be except a series of superstitions? And why promote them? It's clear they do that because they are thinking of regional folklore, and, of course, all the regional and all the national have prestige in this curious epoch. It seems that such-and-such a region is very important. For me, it isn't. I try to be worthy of that antique ambition of the stoics—to be a citizen of the world. I do not particularly insist on having been born in the Parish of Saint Nicholas, of the city of Buenos Aires.

FERRARI. It continues, saying: 'They can be substituted by a sociology of literature . . . '

BORGES. Really, I don't know what the sociology of literature can be. If it were a science, it could predict things but, curiously, that sociology is applied to literature which has already happened or which is wanted to happen. This reminds me of a joke by Heine who said: 'The historian, the retrospective prophet.' And that was, perhaps, bettered, curiously, by Juan Valera who said: 'History is the art of prophesizing the past.' Which is certain.

Moreover, I don't know if that sociology of literature will give us the names and, why not, the dates and titles of the great books of the twenty-first century. We are told, rather, that what has happened was inevitable: I believe that nobody could have predicted that in the year 1855, a journalist from Brooklyn would publish *Leaves of Grass* and that would modify all subsequent literature. Or that some years earlier, Edgar Allan Poe, by virtue of those five stories that he wrote, which we all remember: 'The Murders in the Rue Morgue', 'The Purloined Letter', 'The Gold Bug' and the others—nobody could predict that he was going to create a literary genre, the crime genre. And that this genre was going to have such illustrious exponents, well, like Dickens, Wilkie Collins, Chesterton, Eden Philpotts, and like so many others, the list would be interminable, Nicholas Blake . . . well, very many in all parts of the world. I myself with Bioy Casares have tried out that genre in the 'Six Problems for Don Isidro Parodi'. All that would not have happened if Poe had not written those five stories which came to be perfect examples and which tried to determine the laws that would be later fixed, that is to say, the fact of shying away from all violence, of making a crime to be the result of meditation and by observation, and not as unusual police behaviour, through receiving reports.

FERRARI. We arrive then at the two last possibilities . . .

BORGES. Which are?

FERRARI. They can be substituted by sociolinguistics and psycho-linguistics.

BORGES. Good, I can't say anything about those things, since for me they are mere neologisms, and I don't even know if they correspond to disciplines. In any case, they would be such recent disciplines that for many they would be hypothetical. Why prefer to the aesthetic taste the study of those disciplines whose very name is arid?

FERRARI. Your letter ends by saying that, according to fame, the Argentinians are ingenuous . . .

BORGES. That wants to say that possibly many people believe that list is authentic, and some that the danger is serious, that is to say, that it's going to replace literature, the taste for literature, by disciplines about literature. But that is not impossible—I have been a professor for some twenty years, and many students, then, asked me for bibli-ography. I said no, that I'd give them nothing, since bibliography is posterior to the work of a writer. I don't believe that Shakespeare would have read, well, the vast libraries they have written about him. In other words, first is the work. But now so much is written about the work, about the books, and they write about what they have writ-ten, and they write about what they write about what they write . . . that people in general never get to the text, because there is that nui-sance of the bibliography. And that, well, that will continue. Samuel Butler has already said that, with time, the catalogues of the British Museum would not fit in the world. (*Both laugh*) He doesn't even refer to the books, since the catalogues would be too many. That is to say, we are obstructed by the erudition, that is one of the dangers of our time, although there are so many ignorant people. Because the erudite are usually ignorant, or usually only know the point that they studied. The general public—no, it is too vague for them.

FERRARI. In that case, one is dealing with erudition bringing creativity to a close.

BORGES. Yes, perhaps one of the advantages of studying, for example, the origins of literature is that they have lost all that empty talk . . . the names of the authors . . . something so important for actual critics, like the changes of domicile . . . I've read a book about Poe, by Harvey Allen I think, that was no other thing than the changes of Poe's domicile. There was almost nothing else. Nevertheless, the least important are changes of domicile—everybody changes domicile. But the important thing is what a writer has dreamt and the books he has left us. All that is substituted by changes of domicile or—in the case of psychoanalysts—by gossip, indiscretions about sexual life . . . it is understood that every writer must hate his father and love his mother, or hate his mother and love his father. All that is re-emplaced in literature to aesthetic taste which is almost unknown now. Well, I don't know if we really run the risk of what I have spoken, I hope not, I hope to have been personally deceived. I expect a declaration from a person linked to the university saying that—I use then a phrase I believe necessary—that eccentric catalogue does not exist and will not be taken seriously. It would be very sad, moreover, that the university—of course it is usual to exaggerate the importance of the university—dedicates itself to replace literature by mere sociology. But, everything is to be feared in this epoch.

FERRARI. I think that the content of your letter, Borges, has been completely explained.

BORGES. It would be convenient, I think, were other letters by other writers to appear because, maybe, this danger is not imaginary. Perhaps it is real. In that case, it would be convenient if other writers protested. I don't want to mention names, but with a person linked to the university, to deny—it should suffice. And if there are other writers who want to express their alarm faced with this unlikely but nor impossible danger, so much the better.

Boileau said: 'The certain may, sometimes, not be verisimilar.' And in this case, it can be treated as a certain fact, and as implausible as I have thought, or as I try to think.

FERRARI. Or the contrary.

BORGES. Yes. Everything is possible.

25

W. B. Yeats (I)

●

OSVALDO FERRARI. I know that years ago, Borges, you have spoken about an Irish poet, whom you admire, in the Argentinean Association of English Culture. I'm referring to William Butler Yeats.

JORGE LUIS BORGES. Yes, of course, it's a pleasant theme. Eliot believed that Yeats was the maximum poet of this century. He had that opinion, and I think I share it, although for me, personally, I like more another type of poetry—I like more the type of poetry of Frost, or of Browning. The poetry of Yeats is, as you know, for saying, verbal, but all poetry is verbal. In the case of Yeats, like the case of his compatriot Joyce, one notes more than emotion the love of words, a kind of sensuality of words. And that his verses impress us, let's say, as verbal objects beyond what they want to say. We have an example in this country too, the most obvious would be Lugones, don't you think? Or in Castilian literature, Quevedo or Góngora correspond to that verbal sensuality, the love of words. Now Yeats is a much more passionate poet than Quevedo, but he shares with him that verbal sensuality, that verbal emotion. For example: 'That dolphin-torn, that gong-tormented sea'. If I translate: 'Ese mar desgarrado de delfines, ese mar atornmentado de gongs', I think that nothing survives. We are facing gibberish, trying to imagine what one wants to say. But when one finds in English 'that dolphin-torn, that gong-tormented sea' one feels wounded, wounded by beauty, immediately, and the explanation is the least of it.

FERRARI. We must be guided by the sound of the words.

BORGES. Yes, but maybe that can be applied to all poetry—the important would come to be the cadences, the sound of the words. The sense can not exist, or can be doubtful. That is the least of it, it seems to me.

Now, I have looked for an extreme example from Yeats, and not all the poetry of Yeats corresponds to that type of expression although he has written many poems of admirable mention, of admirable argument. Now, curiously, he began by the 'Celtic twilight', what was called 'The Celtic penumbra'. That is to say, he made verses voluntarily vague—they were, above all, auditory, and visual. Later he left that type of poetry, nostalgic, languid, and wrote a very direct poetry and re-wrote his first poems. All that nostalgia, sentiment— he came to abominate the sentimental, and to write a very direct poetry. And in the last of his verses, he avoided what can seem too deliberately literary. For example, in a version of a poem, he had put 'That star-laden sky', 'Ese cielo cargado de estrellas'. Which is false for the northern hemisphere, and is true for the southern, since ours, the sky of this hemisphere, is more laden with stars. Now with a phrase like 'star-laden' one feels immediately like something completely impossible in the oral language, something that corresponds to the written . . . and that later he tried to leave although he continued being very attentive to the force of each word.

FERRARI. It's said that in those early times, when he was young, the fundamental influences were Shelley, Spencer and the pre-Raphaelite atmosphere.

BORGES. Yes, but I think that the pre-Raphaelites did it better than those of the 'Celtic twilight'. Rosetti, for example, there's a precision in Rosetti . . . well, and in Morris there is something else, but I believe all that poetry had an obvious master—Tennyson. Although, maybe, those who followed him did it better than he. I think that case is not rare, the case of disciples who exceed their master.

FERRARI. Who better their master.

BORGES. Yes. Moreover, why not suppose there is division of labour— there is a poet who invents a rhetoric, and there are others who use it, and who use it better than he. I should say that among ourselves the classic case would be that of Ezequiel Martínez Estrada. I think Ezequiel Martínez Estrada is inconceivable without Lugones and without Rubén Darío. But I think that if we forget that consideration, which is merely historical, chronological, and if we take a poem, the best poem, let's say, of each one, the best would be that of Martínez Estrada who was later.

FERRARI. Yes, also amazing as a prose writer.

BORGES. Who . . . Martínez Estrada?

FERRARI. Yes, I don't know if you share it.

BORGES. No, I don't—I think his prose is, rather, a journalist's prose. In exchange, his poetry, no—his poetry, it seems to me, is true poetry. Now, he was in agreement with you because he said his poetry wasn't worth anything.

FERRARI. What's curious is that who most concerns himself with praising Martínez Estrada's poetry in the country is you, Borges. Because everyone else speaks almost exclusively of his prose.

BORGES. Nevertheless, if you published books called *Radiography of the Pampas*, we cannot expect much of that prose, could we? Good. He also wrote a book of verses called *Puppets with Light Feet*, a title which augurs nothing good and which is more like a threat. However, here you have some splendid poems: the poem to Whitman, the poem to Emerson, the poem to Poe, which he calls 'Three Stars to the Great Bear', the title he gives them. Then he has some about Spanish poets also, the section is called 'Spanish Towers', and there, for example, are sometimes stanzas which seem to repeat studiously the errors of Lugones.

We've got away from Yeats.

FERRARI. Yes, I wanted to tell you that in the case of Yeats, there's a constant in his poems—the preoccupation with Ireland. You will remember, for example, the last which he called 'Under Ben Bullen', a kind of poetic testament to Ireland. And, before, that other poem 'A Vision'.

BORGES. Yes. He has other themes which are personal. For example, that tower, which he has, with a spiral staircase. There's a very strange poem of his in which he appears in the tower, the upper chamber of the tower is lit up, and then there are two characters, who are characters of his poems, who meet at the foot of the tower. They converse and one of them says he has found what Yeats had been looking for. And then they speak of him, and they look, and they see that the tower's light has been switched off. And at that moment the poem ends and they leave, because, clearly, they in that moment are being created by the poet who is writing by the light of that lamp which goes out. It's very strange, that argument, isn't it?

FERRARI. Certainly.

BORGES. Yes, very curious. I can't remember what the poem is called, but there are many verses of Yeats in my memory. And then, the contrast, well, between him, an old man . . . it seems, he led a very chaste youth. But later, being old, he felt nostalgia for that turbulent youth . . .

FERRARI. That he didn't have.

BORGES. That he didn't have, but that he felt.

26

W. B. Yeats (II)

●

OSVALDO FERRARI. Many times, Borges, when we talk about the spirit or the muse, you recall a concept of Yeats—that of 'the great memory'.

JORGE LUIS BORGES. Yes, one supposes that Yeats invented that concept in order to justify his life, well, his chaste youth and his lack of direct experience of, let's say, physical love. Then Yeats invented that immediate experiences are unnecessary since all individuals inherit 'the great memory' and that memory will be the memory of the species. Or more concretely, the memory that is inherited from all that has been lived by the parents, the grandparents, the great grandparents, and so on, in geometric progression, almost infinitely. And that is 'the great memory', a sort of vast deposit of memories that every individual inherits on being born. But, later, in years of maturity and old age, he liked to think about his personal memory which was of a fictitious past. That is what we all do with the past—what we imagine does not correspond exactly with what we lived.

FERRARI. Or what poets do.

BORGES. Yes, what poets do. And then Yeats created a memory, let's say, of lovers ignorant of everything except their love and their immediate experiences. And he said: Wisdom is corporal decrepitude, physical decrepitude. When we were young, we loved and were ignorant. But that corresponded to a false memory of his, and is one of the themes of his poetry.

FERRARI. That seems like Wilde's phrase, as regards experience: It is the name we give to our errors, to the knowledge of our errors.

BORGES. Yes, it has some link. I think Yeats considerably overestimated the value of Wilde's 'The Ballad of Reading Gaol'. To me it seems a very imperfect ballad and full of false features. For example, when Wilde compares clouds, he compares them with ships that have silver sails. And that seems completely alien to what a prisoner can think, it seems completely false. The theme itself seems false to me, that consciousness of death as a presence which encircles the condemned, I don't believe that . . . in any case, it doesn't seem realistic. And neither does the language—at times a cultured language, at times deliberately popular, and the mixture isn't happy. But I should say Wilde's great work is his poetry, well, we could call it decorative. But not the ballad which seems to keep itself halfway between the realism of Kipling's ballads and the fantastical of other ballads, for example, the famous ballad of Coleridge's ancient mariner, which is purely fantastical.

FERRARI. Now, dealing with Yeats, there is an aspect which would perhaps explain, within his poetry, things that, if we did not know what interested him, for example, particularly theosophy, we could not discover. For example, you will recall 'A Vision', probably inspired by occult philosophy and in the mysticism which he cultivated.

BORGES. No, I don't remember that poem.

FERRARI. But you recall that he frequented Madame Blavatsky's circle.

BORGES. Yes, he belonged to that society called 'The Golden Dawn', only known here by a line of Rubén Darío: 'But it is mine the golden dawn'. And one supposes that 'the golden dawn' means to say youth, adolescence. But, well, doubtless he used it in that sense but he took the phrase 'the golden dawn' from the circle of Madame Blavatsky, didn't he? The author of *Isis*, one of the books Güiraldes read and reread.

FERRARI. Yes, there's another book titled *Isis* by Villiers de L'Isle Adam.

BORGES. Oh, good. I think there's a mention of *Isis* in *The World as Will und Idea* by Schopenhauer. I think the text is taken from Plutarch. And he speaks of an image of Isis who says: 'I am all what is, all what was, all what will be, and no one has lifted my veil.'

FERRARI. Ah, it is very lovely.

BORGES. Good, and that Schopenhauer linked with a much more beautiful phrase which is in Diderot's 'Jack le fataliste': Jack and his master who lived in an immense castle arrive, and on the facade of the castle is written something such as 'You are here before arriving, and when you leave, you will remain here.' It is the same idea but it is better said. Schopenhauer notes as extraordinary the appearance of that phrase in 'Jack le fataliste'. Possibly invented by Diderot, or read in an ancient text, since in that epoch quotations without inverted commas were permitted, weren't they? On the contrary, they were done in order to be recognized by the reader—not to deceive the reader. The one who has written a defence possibly of the quotations and, why not, of the plagiarisms also, is Alfonso Reyes. And of the allusions. He says they are all a wink at the reader.

FERRARI. A sign of understanding.

BORGES. Yes, that is to say, a phrase is quoted not to deceive, not to imitate an ancient author but so that the reader shares that memory with the writer.

FERRARI. Clearly, perhaps that theosophical inclination of Yeats explains why in many of his poems we find myths—for example, the Celtic legends.

BORGES. Yes. Curiously, in the same way, to cite the most famous case, *The Divine Comedy*, in which we find what we can call 'Christian mythology' along with Greek mythology. For example, in Hell is the Minotaur, there are centaurs. Obviously, that does not belong to 'Christian mythology', to which belong, I don't know, the saints or, well, virgins, or whatever. In equal manner, Yeats combined Celtic mythology with Greek mythology. And in his best sonnet, one of the best sonnets of the English language—in other words, one of the world's best sonnets—the sonnet 'Leda and the Swan'. It's a theme that has been dealt with many times, but in the Yeats poem it is treated in another way, right from the first verse. Because painters and poets have figured Leda seated beside the sea, or by a lake, and the swan calmly navigating towards her. In exchange, in Yeats case: no, the bird, who one imagines enormous, the great swan is also Zeus. He falls from the sky and knocks Leda down.

Now, there's a moment in which he says 'The feathered glory', doesn't he?—he knocks her down and there is a moment when the two are one. When the bird, who is also Zeus, possesses her. And then Yeats imagines that, in that moment, she too is in some way Zeus. That is to say, she knows the past, the present and the future. And in that moment, since Leda is the mother of Helen, in that moment he says: 'Troy is burning.' In that moment, before the indifferent beak releases her, because the beak is at once a bird and the god, she sees all—she sees the wall of Troy burning and she sees Agamemnon dead. And he asks if, at the same time, she feels the power of the god, the passion of the god she possessed, maybe, the wisdom of the god too, before the indifferent beak lets her fall.

That sonnet is one of the last of Yeats, and it appears that it was dictated to his secretary who was duly scandalized, faced by the theme. Curiously, there's an earlier poem by Dante Gabriel Rossetti, whose scheme is the same, because he proceeds by referring to the story of Helen, but in that ancient present, which is now the past, he sees the future which is now also a past. Then, while narrating Helen's history he foresees the fact . . . well, the theme of the poem is the fact that Paris is enamoured by her, and in this moment in which Paris is enamoured by her, Troy is condemned, Troy is burning, and he says 'High Troy is in flames.' In other words, both things are mixed.

FERRARI. The myth anticipates reality.

BORGES. Yes, the myth anticipates reality and, doubtless, Yeats knew that poem, he imitated it and went beyond it in his poem about Leda and the swan, since they are the same symbols also—Helen and Troy. All that has been one time. Those two times so far from the time, a present and a future, still remote but given simultaneously.

FERRARI. Good. We could here record Yeats' liking for and dedication to the theatre, because in some way the scenes are at once theatrical.

BORGES. Yes, they are theatrical, although in that case it is a sonnet.

FERRARI. Yes, I was referring to the scenes.

BORGES. Yes, but that could have been a theme for the theatre also. And maybe even more efficaciously, if one can be more efficacious than those sonnets of Yeats.

FERRARI. I don't think so.

BORGES. I doubt it too. For Yeats both mythologies were equally vivid—the Celtic, which he had studiously learnt, and the Greek, which is inherited naturally by all poets now, isn't it? Differently from others which require special study—the Scandinavian, for example, or better said, the Irish which Wagner studied in Germany. It came from the ultimate Thule, from distant Ireland.

FERRARI. Yeats was interested in Japanese theatre.

BORGES. Yes, because he saw in that theatre, a theatre that was, let's say, voluntary and almost ostentatiously artificial. A theatre which in no moment tries to look like what we call reality, the everyday. He saw that theatre . . . well, I've seen it—seen is a metaphor in my case—but I have attended representations of Japanese theatre, and at the beginning they were almost insupportable, for the slowness, for the music, completely foreign to me.

FERRARI. In Japan?

BORGES. In Japan, yes. It had been decided that I should spend an hour seeing that theatre but, without wanting to, we were all morning, all afternoon, and even by night, seeing it. And I in the end . . . I wasn't able to explain intellectually what I saw, but it began to win me over. And the slowness, the curious slowness of the actors. For example, it is understood that an actor has, well, to have his arm near his chin. But then he has to lower it, slowly . . . and that can last ten minutes. Extreme slowness, and with voices which seemed to us at times terrible. And all that the public follows because the room is lit up, the persons have scores and the script, and they are following it. The piece of theatre, which everybody knows by heart, and they continue following, continue observing how the actor is interpreting . . . and there are famous actors . . .

FERRARI. All different, and original.

BORGES. Yes, different and original. Nevertheless, the people know them by heart.

FERRARI. I mean, original in relation to Western theatre.

BORGES. Oh yes. Talking of that: I attended some days ago at a performance of *Macbeth* by Orson Welles, and I observed how Welles deliberately omitted the most famous verses because he knew they were already in the reader's memory, that the reader anticipated them and that it isn't necessary that he speak them.

FERRARI. Of course. I can't omit a date, that it is produced around 1923, when perhaps that distinction was more serious than it now is—they gave the Nobel Prize to Yeats. You will remember.

BORGES. No, the year '23 I associate with a fact much less important, to a negligible fact—the publication of my first book.

FERRARI. *Fervor de Buenos Aires.*

BORGES. Possibly, in the year '23 I did not have greater notice of Yeats, it's most likely. The news will have reached me later.

FERRARI. It's possible, clearly.

BORGES. Of course, things happen gradually and slowly and anachronistically, like facts.

27

The Literary Thinker

●

OSVALDO FERRARI. It has seemed wrong to me the idea of those who think you are not a thinker, by having less to do with philosophy than with literature.

JORGE LUIS BORGES. Well, philosophy is, let's say, a conjunction of doubt, of vacillations. An Argentinean professor, whose name I don't wish to remember, made students study by a type of catechism and forced them to answer exactly, word for word. That is to say, they had to learn by heart—they did not have to understand it, or to think about variations. And the first question was: 'What is philosophy?' and you had to answer exactly thus: 'Knowledge clear and precise.' Not precise and clear. Now that is evidently false. If I say to you that the continuation of Peru Street is called Florida and the continuation of Bolívar is called San Martín, one is dealing with knowledge clear and precise, of scant or null philosophical value. How rare that some-one who drafts a text does not take account of that, no? Well, he will have done it with much of a rush, and later it is demanded that it be repeated. If they say to him 'knowledge precise and clear'—no, sir, not precise and clear, clear and precise, you have not studied, have you? (*Both laugh*) He was a professor of philosophy in the Faculty of Philosophy and Letters in the University of Buenos Aires, and he began committing so obvious a logical error, as scandalous as that. How is philosophy going to be clear and precise knowledge? It is knowledge of doubts and contradictory explanations.

FERRARI. He began in an anti-philosophical manner.

BORGES. But, of course, yes. How is the history of philosophy going to be clear and precise knowledge? No, one learns that there have been, well, I don't know, five or five thousand thinkers who have considered the universe or life in a manner completely different. From the moment in which there are philosophical schools and in which there is a name by which they have distinguished, one is not dealing with knowledge clear and precise. One is dealing with a series of doubts. I remember De Quincey said that to have discovered a problem is not less important than to have discovered a solution. Which is good.

FERRARI. It is very good. But you have established what I would call a literary thought which approximates to the truth or to reality in a distinct manner. Your vision of destiny, particularly of predestination which underlies the life of each one, contrasting it with chance, for example.

BORGES. Yes, but that belief in predestination doesn't mean that there is someone who knows it. It means, rather, that there is a mechanism, well, a merciless mechanism. That is to say, that if each instant is determined by the previous instant, there is a mechanism, isn't there? But that doesn't mean to say there may be someone who knows it or who foresaw it. It means there is something that is operating beyond us, or perhaps we are that operation. Of course, that is also a conjecture, since it cannot be proved.

FERRARI. But exactly, it is conjectured, differently from the professor you knew.

BORGES. Yes.

FERRARI. Now, you also used to refer to the ordered or to the cosmic as a counterpoint to chaos.

BORGES. Of course, since cosmos is order and chaos would be the contrary. In passing, I don't know if we have spoken of the word cosmetic, whose origin is in cosmos, and wants to say small order, the small cosmos that a person imposes on his or her face. The root is the same, so that I, for example, who does not use cosmetics would be chaotic, no? (*Both laugh*) Now, one also says that consciousness, from within, goes on moulding the face.

FERRARI. Oh, how good is that!

BORGES. Yes, and I remember a phrase that they attribute to Lincoln. He needed a secretary, and they brought him a series of photographs, and he looked at one of them and said no. And someone replied: But this gentleman is not responsible for his face. And Lincoln said to him: Having lived thirty years, each man is responsible for his face. Which comes to be the same idea. And when one says 'the face is the mirror of the soul'—it comes to be the same, doesn't it? except it's being said in a less dramatic manner. 'Each man is responsible for his face.'

FERRARI. The Greeks said it and Leonardo da Vinci said it.

BORGES. The face, yes.

FERRARI. Now, you used to refer to what in our epoch seems to have been lost—a possible meaning ordered to something superior or cosmic. It would seem that our mode of life is to live in whatever manner.

BORGES. And the result is in full view. I think there is no doubt. Now that we approach the end of this century, I have the impression that it is poor compared with the nineteenth century. And perhaps the nineteenth was poor compared with the eighteenth. However, I already know that division into centuries is arbitrary, and that a century maybe must be judged by the following, that it has been introduced by the previous, hasn't it? So that a strong argument against the nineteenth is that it produced the twentieth. A strong argument against the eighteenth is that it produced the nineteenth. Although that division into centuries is completely arbitrary, it seems that thought needs these conventions.

FERRARI. That division of time.

BORGES. Yes, it seems that it is necessary to divide, although we know that generalizations are false. Which is a generalization in its turn, of course.

FERRARI. You said a little while ago that one of the things whose loss is lamentable is the Christian sense of good and evil in our epoch.

BORGES. Well, not only Christian, since the sense of good and evil is previous to Christianity, the ethic . . .

FERRARI. Is in Plato, for example.

BORGES. Yes, good, and the word 'ethical' was professed by Aristotle who did not have to have, well, a prophetic knowledge of Christianity. I think it's an instinct that everyone has. When we work, we know if we are working well or badly. Beyond the consequences that can be beneficial or detrimental or satanic.

FERRARI. However, how could you support an ethic which had nothing to do with good and evil? Could you have an ethic only with a legal sense, for example?

BORGES. No. If we have read 'Billy Budd', we know we can't, since that admirable story by Melville deals with the conflict between justice and the law. The law is an attempt, well, to codify justice, but it often fails, which is natural.

FERRARI. You seem to have for the ethical a superior appreciation, in the sense that, I think, for you, it could be more important to possess an ethic than to possess a religion.

BORGES. To possess a religion is to possess an ethic, well, an ethic helped or hindered by a mythology.

FERRARI (*laughs*). Yes . . .

BORGES. Good. In Japan, I think there is that idea, since, for example, the emperor, and perhaps everyone, are Shintoists and Buddhists. Nevertheless, they are two beliefs very, very distinct. Buddhism is a philosophy and Shintoism is a belief in a type of pantheism. Since there are eight million gods, who go from one side to the other, we can suspect that *Omnia sunt plena Jovis*, all things are full of Jupiter, or full of divinity, as Virgil wrote.

I think there was a discussion between Jesuits and protestant ministers who could have been Evangelists or Methodists, or whatever, about the number of converts they had garnered. And they did a statistical analysis and discovered that those converts were the same. That is to say, the persons were Buddhists, Shintoists, Catholics, Protestants, Mormons maybe. It was understood that all religions were facets of the same truth, so that religions turned out to be diverse facets of the ethic. Of course, the ethic is different in each case, or is not completely equal.

FERRARI. This seems to me a thought very much your own, Borges. The extension of the ethical to the religious or the religious as a member of the ethical. You once said that the importance in a dialogue is the spirit of investigation.

BORGES. Yes, for that the idea of, well damn it, unfortunately it's found in Plato also, the idea that someone wins in a discussion is an error, because what does it matter? If one manages to discover a truth, it little matters if it comes from A, from B, from C, from D or from E. The important thing is to arrive at that truth or to investigate that possible truth. But in general, one sees conversation as a polemic, right? That is to say, it's understood that one person loses and another gains, which is a way of obstructing truth or of making it impossible. That mere personal vanity of being right. Why want to be right? The important thing is to reach being right, and if someone can help us, so much the better.

FERRARI. Now, this preoccupation with the truth, it seems to me more a preoccupation of philosophers than of artists. Artists seem to preoccupy themselves with finding reality, what Plato called 'the real reality'.

BORGES. Yes, but I don't know if there is essentially a difference.

FERRARI. Clearly.

BORGES. I think a writer must be ethical, in the sense that if he narrates a dream, if he narrates a fable, if he narrates a fantastic story or a story of science-fiction, he must believe in that dream. That is to say, he knows that historically it is not real but it has to be something that his imagination accepts. And the reader, moreover, takes account of whether his imagination accepts it or not, since a reader immediately discovers the insincerities of a work. I think that someone, reading something, takes account of whether the author has imagined it or if, simply, he is playing with words. I think that is felt immediately if one is a good reader. I am not sure about being a good writer, but I believe myself to be a good reader (*laughs*) which is more important, since, well, one dedicates a small part of time to writing and a lot to reading. Even in my case, even though I can't do it directly. Neither of the two things. I have to do it through other eyes and other voices.

FERRARI. I dissent with you as to the first part, I believe you are equivalent in the two operations.

BORGES. Talking of reading, I remember how I always return to it, the *Quixote*. Well, to judge by what Cervantes recounts, the only thing that happens to Alonso Quijano were his books. Of course, there's a vague love for Aldonza Lorenzo, there's the eventual friendship with Sancho, a friendship always discussed and not always easy, and it appears the Don Quixote had no infancy. We get to know him when he is fifty years old and the first thing that we know is that he was a reader.

FERRARI. Certainly.

BORGES. And it seems that books were the most important thing that happened in all his life, since the decision that Alonso Quijano takes to convert himself into Don Quixote, well, it comes from Amadis de Gaula, from Palmerín of England, from the novels of chivalry that he had read.

FERRARI. Faith and the lack of faith, Borges, could be, perhaps, two personal roads, two forms of approaching the truth.

BORGES. Yes, I think to have faith, essentially. That is to say, I have faith in ethics, and I have faith in the imagination also, even in my imagination. But I have above all faith in the imagination of others, in those who have taught me to imagine. Now, Blake believed that salvation was triple: the first example would be that of Jesus who believed that salvation is ethical. That is to say, that a man is saved by his works. Later, we have Swedenborg, the Swede, who adds the idea of intellectual salvation. And then comes Blake, Swedenborg's rebel disciple, and he says that salvation also has to be aesthetic. Now, as he thought about Jesus, he believed that Jesus had taught also the aesthetic salvation by means of his parables. That, already, the fact that Jesus did not express himself through reason but through parables . . . parables that were works of art. So he said that Christ had taught both intellectual salvation and aesthetic salvation. He thought that the man who saves himself from everything is the one who saves himself ethically, intellectually and aesthetically. That is to say, every man has to be an artist.

28

Time

●

OSVALDO FERRARI. You have many times occupied yourself, Borges, with the idea of time, or with the perception of time that different thinkers have had.

JORGE LUIS BORGES. Yes.

FERRARI. And in one of our conversations, you got to express that time is more real than us, or that our substance is time, that we are made of time.

BORGES. I'm convinced of that, which is a form of idealism, since for the materialists the essential is space, the essential are, let's say, the atoms. And in exchange, for the idealist—no, the essential is that dreaming we call time, it is the cosmic process, and not the fact that among our many experiences are space and time.

FERRARI. I see.

BORGES. So that when I say that our substance is time, I mean to say that I am an idealist, that I think that what is important is that succession of before, during, after—that is the essential. Now, we could think that dreaming is impersonal. In other words, just as one says 'it rains' and there's no subject of the rain, simply, it's raining, it is falling water, we can think of dreaming without a dreamer.

FERRARI. Oh, of course.

BORGES. That is to say, it's a verb without an active subject. But that is difficult for people to accept, it appears impossible for them for that to happen. Nevertheless, it was able to be. There's a phrase of Shaw which I've often repeated: 'God is in the making', God is making himself. And that making itself of time would be what is called the cosmic process or, in a more modest manner, universal history. All the cosmic process, without excluding our conversation this evening, and the fact that there are persons who are dreaming, living other things—well, that would be that 'making itself' of God. Now, an important consequence of that phrase of Shaw would be that God would not be a being that had already existed or who is existing. God is, in any case for us, in the future, and not in the past. In other words, all the cosmic process goes towards God.

FERRARI. It's Rilke's idea, of course.

BORGES. We are going towards God. Scotus Eriugena and others earlier thought that in the beginning it is God, that then God branched out, let's say, in all his creatures: minerals, vegetables, animals, also humans. But then universal history concluded that all these beings came back to being God. There's a very lovely poem by Victor Hugo which is called—and the title is already a poem—'Ce que dit la bouche d'ombre' ('What the Mouth of the Shadow Says'). And it is a kind of resumé of universal history. And in the end he supposes all creatures come back to God. And this would be in accord with the idea that the devil also returns to God, that evil becomes a being part of the cosmic process. Now, Hugo saw it in his manner, in his visual manner, he saw the monsters, the leviathans, dragons, the sombre angel, the black angel, Satan, and all of them returning to the divinity.

Curiously, perhaps without greater notice of the theology, there is a drama called *Back to Methusalah* by Shaw which also becomes an universal history, since it begins in the Garden of Eden with Adam and Eve. And in the last act, everything returns to the divinity. That is to say, Shaw, without wanting to, would have turned to dream the dream of that other Irishman of the ninth century, Scotus Eriugena, who translated from the Greek of Dionysius the Areopagite, and whose system became exactly the one of Shaw—all of Creation, all creatures start from God, and at the end of a long and intricate process return to the divinity. How strange, those two Irishmen. I don't know if Shaw knew about Eriugena, perhaps not, but the system is the same. The system of Shaw's *Back to Methusalah* is the system of Eriugena's treatise.

FERRARI. How curious!

BORGES. Yes, two Irishmen, and the two with the same vision of the world—a world whose source is God and whose sea, paraphrasing Jorge Manrique, is God also. In other words, it begins with the divinity. We have this actual process, so complicated, with so many discords, so many wars; and then we unite ourselves with the divinity.

Lilith appears in Shaw's drama, and she says that she can see that but she cannot see beyond. So that the universal history which would be the theme of Shaw's drama, in which of course jocular and satirical passages are not lacking, is the return of things to God. Apocatastasis, I believe they say in Greek, but my Greek is fallible. So that it came to be that, and then, of course, our substance would be time or would be God...

FERRARI. It's curious that before, in your essay about the refutations of time . . .

BORGES. Well, that essay was a logical game . . . .

FERRARI. A great game . . .

BORGES. And the proof of that is the title, which is ironic, since it is called 'New Refutation of Time'. Now, if time does not exist, the refutation cannot be new, and it cannot be ancient either. So the title indicates one is dealing with a joke—new, which already implies time, and then: refutation of time, that is to say, the word time is not admitted, the word 'new' is not tolerated, nor the word 'ancient'. Since if there is not time, nothing is new and nothing is recent, or nothing is past, present or future or conjectural either.

FERRARI. However, it responds to a very serious study made by you in that epoch.

BORGES. I don't know if it was very serious, I think it was a logical game, simply. But I took it seriously. In any case, I had it printed . . . Manie Molina Vedina drew an hourglass for the cover, it was never put on sale. Later it was included.

FERRARI. In *Other Inquisitions*. In the introduction, you adhered to the attitude of Juan Crisóstomo Lafinur, in respect of what he called 'to purify the philosophy of theological studies'.

BORGES. I don't remember that phrase. And good, it is a further motive to get closer to my great grand-uncle, Doctor Juan Crisóstomo Lafinur. I think that of my many elders, I have not been able to converse with any of them. For example, how difficult would have been the dialogue with Colonel Isidoro Suárez, or with the General Miguel Estanislao Soler? I think as impossible as the dialogue with other officers, no? But Juan Crisóstomo Lafinur was a poet, he wrote that . . . beautiful elegy for the death of Belgrano which contains at least some happy verses, and was, as Gutíerrez said, the classic poet of the romantic movement, before Echeverría. His verses are at once romantic and classical. It is rare to find euphonic verses like those written in this country, in 1820. It seems very unusual, since the poets completely lacked an ear, to judge by another of my forefathers, Luis de Tejada, who wrote a book whose title is beautiful although a bit terrible, *The Pilgrim in Babylonia*. Unfortunately, it was not limited to the title—he wrote the poem, cacophonous and ridiculous.

But we have moved away from time, which is more important than Juan Crisóstomo Lafinur.

FERRARI. I said that, differently from Juan Crisóstomo Lafinur, you in recent times do not let the religious or mystical vision be included in your thought, as we saw earlier in Shaw and others.

BORGES. Is it that one really needs a religion? Difficult are the dogmas. Therefore I believe I could be, with many difficulties, a Buddhist, since Buddhism does not demand mythology. Buddhism demands belief in the ethical, maybe in transmigration, but certainly in the ethical, and does not impose any mythology. So much so that I had a discussion with a Japanese painter, Kazuya Sakai—I knew that he was Buddhist—and I spoke, well, of the fact that Buddha was born in Nepal some five hundred years before the Christian era. And he was very angry with me because he denied the historicity of the Buddha. In other words, the importance is the doctrine—and not whether the Buddha had existed. On the other hand, Christianity imposes a very difficult mythology on us. To suppose that God may have condescended to become a man, to suppose that the sacrifice of God on the cross may have saved all of us, that a man can save himself by an alien sacrifice. All that is very, very difficult.

FERRARI. Too anthropological?

BORGES. Too difficult. On the other hand, Buddhism, well, you can accept. In Japan, you can be Shintoist. That is to say, you can believe in eight million gods. Moreover, in the doctrine of the Buddha, you can do without gods. Catholicism demands so much mythology—that of a personal god, and, worse a god who is three. That already goes beyond my credulity though it is very large. If God is the Father and the Son, it means that for thirty-three years he took some holiday on earth, did he not? Because he went on being God in heaven at the same time he was a man on earth, and he knew the tastes and the sorrows of the human condition. And what's more, the physical pain of the cross. All this seems an impossible conception, at least for me.

FERRARI. Clearly,. In whatever case, there is a very big difference between what theology proposes and what faith proposes.

BORGES. Oh, I think so.

FERRARI. There are those who think that theology has to do with the decline of faith, because it deals with the moment in which faith needs to explain itself to its very self.

BORGES. A thing that has been said, it has often been observed, is that in India there are no proofs of the transmigration of souls, because people spontaneously believe in transmigrations.

FERRARI. That is faith.

BORGES. In exchange, there are I think four or five proofs of the existence of God. Which proves that theologians are not very sure, doesn't it? Because if something is proved, it is because proof is needed. If I say three and four are seven, and you don't understand, nothing has happened. But if you understand, then there's no need to look for examples. You don't need to have proof, well, with chess pieces, with cards, with animals, with persons, with books, with houses—no, it's not necessary. It would be rare that they say to you: They have discovered some stones on the moon, and three and four are not seven. Well, I have written a story about that, that there are some stories that are added, are subtracted, are multiplied, but which don't give a fixed number. But those are magic objects imagined by that story, nothing more. That story is titled 'Blue Tigers'.

FERRARI. Ah, yes. In any case, it seems important to me to differentiate theology and faith.

BORGES. Yes, because theology came to be a reasoning of faith..

FERRARI. Almost something alien to faith.

BORGES. Yes, alien to faith, since it supposes that faith is earlier.

FERRARI. Of course.

BORGES. Now, St Anselm, who invented ontological proof, personally believed. But he prayed to God, saying: 'There are people who do not believe in your existence, and I should like to have proof in order to convince them and, consequently, to save their souls.'

FERRARI. Not in order to convince himself.

BORGES. No. Then God gave him ontological proof—the most fallible of all, I think.

FERRARI. In those refutations of yours about time, one of the most arduous was the conclusion about whether the world was real. And you deduced, among other things, if the world is real, then you are Borges.

BORGES. Ah, it's certain, yes—a melancholy conclusion, of course (*laughs*).

FERRARI (*laughs*). I don't think so.

BORGES. I should prefer to be some other, but if I were some other, I should prefer not to be that some other, wouldn't I? Everybody is, unfortunately, an I, or thinks of being an I, which is the same. Now, what is the I?—that we don't know. I read that Buddhist catechism: 'The questions of the king Milinda'. Milinda is a Hindu distortion of Menandro. And the first article, that is to say, the first thing that the king's priest says to him is that the I does not exist. It is the first article of faith for the Buddhists—that the I does not exist. That was later maintained by Hume, Schopenhauer; Macedonio Fernández among us, the negation of the I. And I have come to believe that the I does not exist—which is a contradiction, no?.

217

FERRARI. Clearly.

BORGES. Since I am the one who has reached that conclusion, and not the neighbour.

FERRARI. Inevitably, Borges is going to end being Borges.

BORGES. It appears so, I'm very sorry. (*Both laugh*) But if there are transmigrations of the soul, then it will be another. But I shan't know that I have been Borges in the previous existence, and I shall be tranquil. I can stop reading my work, which is what I do now, otherwise.

FERRARI. This conclusion at which you have arrived in this conversation about time . . .

BORGES. Time is an infinite theme. It's as infinite as time, isn't it?

FERRARI. Naturally.

BORGES. Since we cannot imagine either the beginning or the end. If we take a first instant, then, what preceded it?

FERRARI. And neither can we conceive, as you have said, eternity.

BORGES. Well, St Augustine found a solution: 'Not in time, but with time, God created earth.' That is to say, the first instant of creation coincides with the first instant of time. Now, I don't know if that is much more than a verbal trick. Maybe not. In any case, it satisfied him while he wrote it, didn't it? It's to say that when God created the world, he created time—the first instant of creation is the first instant of time. But I don't know if anything is resolved with that. I don't know if one invincibly does not think in an instant earlier to the first instant. And that would require another instant, and that another, and thus infinitely.

FERRARI. Infinitely. I remember an earlier time in which we spoke about time, and you came to the conclusion that art and literature must try to liberate themselves from time.

BORGES. Ah, yes, good, it would be a way, it would be an euphemism for saying they tend to try to be eternal. That is to say, contrary to the 'sociology of literature' with which we are now threatened, aren't we? The opposite. Moreover, literature is more important than sociology, since an art is more important than a science. Above all, than a fallible science, invented, perhaps, the day before yesterday.

FERRARI. Of course. It is, furthermore, what Rilke recommended to the poet or the writer: To write as if one were eternal. And I think in some manner . . . I think I see that attitude in you, sometimes.

BORGES. Maybe we are eternal. Everything is possible. There is something in us which is further on from the vicissitudes of our histories. And that one feels when something terrible has happened to one. It has happened to me, for example: a woman left me and I felt desperate. And then I thought: What can it matter to me what happens to a South American writer called Jorge Luis Borges, during the twentieth century? In other words, is there something in me, is there something in my eternal self, that is alien to my circumstances, to my name, and to my adventures and misfortunes? I think we all have felt it, haven't we? And I think that it is a true sentiment, that of a secret root which one carries and which is beyond the successive facts of living.

FERRARI. In that case yes there would be a possibility of eternity, although we may not be conscious of it.

BORGES. And that possibility would not be future—it would be always in us. That is to say, it would be eternal.

FERRARI. Eternity would be contemporaneous.

BORGES. It would be contemporaneous, yes, and what is more, it would border past and future.

●

The translator wishes to thank
Lucy Edkins, Tobias Ray and Jason Wilson
for their patience, helpful advice and assistance.

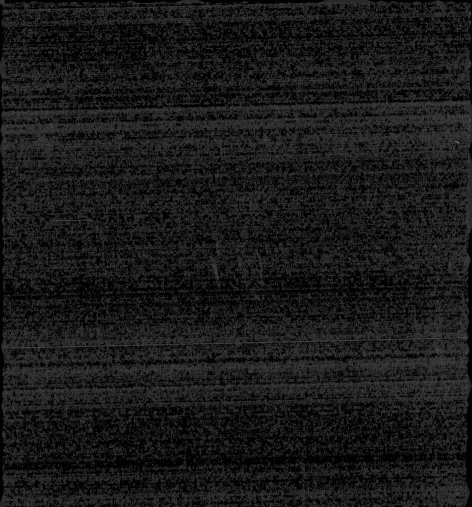